Roger Protz

THE GREAT BRITISH
BEER
BOOK

i
Impact Books

First published in Great Britain 1987
by Impact Books, 112 Bolingbroke Grove,
London SW11 1DA.

BY THE SAME AUTHOR

Pulling a Fast One (What the Brewers Have Done to Your Beer), Pluto Press
Capital Ale, Arrow Books/CAMRA
The Good Beer Guide (editor) 1978 to 1983, CAMRA
Beer, Bed and Breakfast (editor), Robson Books/CAMRA

British Library Cataloguing in Publication Data

Protz, Roger
    The great British beer story.
    1. Beer —— Great Britain —— History
    I. Title
    641.2'3   TP577

    ISBN 0–245–54599–9

Contents

industry. Publican-brewers go into sharp decline and the commercial companies buy up pubs in order to ensure a steady trade for their products.

Chapter Eight: Denting the dustbin

Takeovers and mergers in the 1960s and 1970s reduce drinkers' choice and lead to the switch to mass-produced and heavily promoted keg beers. Drinkers fight back and demand traditional beer through the Campaign for Real Ale.

Chapter Nine: Put the kettle on

From the barley and hop fields to the brewery: a step-by-step guide to brewing and the differences between traditional beer, keg and lager.

Chapter Ten: Raising the living

The large modern public house needed quicker service than pot boys running up and down to the cellar with jugs of beer. The 19th century saw the development of the 'beer engine' triggered by a handpump on the bar to pull beer from the cask.

Chapter Eleven: Signs of the times

Inn signs showed a mainly illiterate nation where ale, victuals and beds were available. Early signs were based on religious terms or used heraldic devices from the nobility. Trades people also had inns and taverns named after their company seals. Kings, queens, politicians and sportsmen have been honoured over the centuries.

Chapter Twelve: Haven't you got homes to go to?

Abbots moaned about monks drinking too much and inns had to close at curfew: from the earliest days of the ale house, the authorities have tried – often without success – to curb drinking. Thanks to David Lloyd George and the Defence of the Realm Act, the English and Welsh are still saddled with pub hours introduced in World War One but relief is now at hand.

Chapter Thirteen: Last orders

A beery voyage of discovery through Britain finds a great profusion of tastes – and the great north-south divide of serving ale with or without a foaming head.

Plain person's guide to pub and beer terms

A glossary that explains the terminology of the brewer and the dedicated drinker

Opening time

This book celebrates a unique type of beer, British beer. The title does not mean that I believe the beer brewed in Britain is better than other countries' brews. There are superb beers brewed in Germany, Belgium, the Netherlands, Czechoslovakia, Denmark and other lands. British beer is different as a result of climate, temperament, insularity and plain cussedness. The heritage of genuine British beer, though, is under threat from a deluge of fake European-style lager that is as much an insult to European master brewers as it is to British tastebuds. The aim of the book is to trace the history of British ale and beer and, it is hoped, to make a small contribution to preserving it for future generations to enjoy.

My thanks go to the Campaign for Real Ale. Without their dedication, zeal and enthusiasm there would have been little left to write about. I am grateful, too, for their permission to reproduce, in amended and updated form, the chapters on how beer is served and the history of pub and inn signs which previously appeared in the *Good Beer Guide*. All the other material is new. My thanks, too, to Charles McMaster of the Scottish Brewing Archive at Heriot-Watt University in Edinburgh for patiently answering my questions and the loan of vital material. Mike Ripley at the Brewers' Society was an inexhaustible fund of knowledge; his work on the exporting of British beer in particular made my chapter on the subject possible. As my relations with the society over the years have tended, at best, to be tepid and for fear that Mr Ripley might be sent to run a home-brew pub in Scapa Flow, I must stress that he is in no way responsible for any of the conclusions in this book.

I have attempted to keep jargon to an absolute minimum but the brewing industry has terms and expressions for the brewing

1

process that may not be familiar to all readers. I have attempted to explain these in the chapter *Put the kettle on* and in the glossary.

Finally, and for reasons which will become immediately clear, my special thanks go to my mother; and also to my wife, Diana, who does not like pubs very much but who does not object when I go to them – the basis, surely, for the perfect relationship.

Roger Protz, April 1987

Oh I have been to Ludlow fair
And left my necktie God knows where,
And carried half way home, or near,
Pints and quarts of Ludlow beer:
Then the world seemed none so bad,
And I myself a sterling lad;
And down in lovely muck I've lain,
Happy till I woke again.

A.E. Housman

CHAPTER ONE

In the beginning was the wort

How the art of ale making came to Britain from Babylon and Egypt, was enjoyed by the locals and by invading Saxons and Danes, was derided by the Romans but became a major activity in hovels, mansions and monasteries.

I started going to pubs at an early age – three to be precise. Flouting the licensing laws and no doubt conniving with the landlord, my mother would smuggle me into the Three Boars in the village of Spooner Row in Norfolk and place me under the bench seat for an hour or two until it was time to take me home to bed. I would stare out in wonder at the smoky room, the noisy, laughing grown-ups and, in particular, the smartly uniformed American servicemen who would press 'candy bars' and giant packets of chewing gum into my willing little hands. If it sounds like a depraved childhood then they were exceptional times, the Second World War seen through the narrow prism of a tiny East Anglian community enlivened by an influx of lonely and generous GIs. My parents, to use the ugly vernacular of the time, had been 'bombed out' in London and mother and small son were 'evacuated' to Norfolk. There was a certain irony in the situation: the Protz family had only arrived in London from Germany in the 1830s but just 100 years on my father dutifully went off to fight an enemy that possibly included some distant relations who in turn may have dropped a bomb with impressive Prussian accuracy on his London home.

My mother, I must hasten to stress, is not a tippler. She is 'respectable' working class and rather looks down on pubs. But in a village whose isolation was deepened by blackout and lack of transport, the pub was the only outlet for entertainment and relaxation. From my little hidey-hole the pub seemed a wondrous place, its excitingly adult atmosphere heightened by the fact that my presence was an illicit one. The pub was owned, I think, by Morgans but it could have been Bullards or Steward and Patteson, the other Norwich brewers. All three are long gone, taken over and closed down by the 'Norwich Brewery

Company', a euphemism for Watneys. If the GIs drank beer then it would have been the local mild and bitter, for there was no lager in those days, not even for crew-cut boys raised on Budweiser and Schlitz. I wonder what they thought of those Norfolk brews, brown, rather warm and flat to their taste and lacking the chill and fizz of their native beers. Like visitors before and after them, they discovered that British beer is different, a difference that often causes confusion. I recalled those times in the Norfolk pub when, some thirty years later, I discovered in Frank Baillie's splendid book, *The Beer Drinker's Companion*, a head-scratching briefing for American servicemen stationed in England during the war. 'The usual English drink is beer,' it said, 'which is not an imitation of German beer, as our beer is, but ale (but they usually call it beer or bitter)'. Ale, beer or bitter, there is no evidence that the GIs took a taste for British beer back from Spooner Row or anywhere else to the US with them.

British beer may seem curious, the odd-ale-out, but it is the type of barley-based fermented drink that all the world enjoyed from pre-Roman times until the industrial revolution. As fundamental changes in manufacturing burst across Europe in the 18th and 19th centuries they solved the problems of continental countries with icy winters and blazing summers. Thermometers, hydrometers, yeast cultivation and refrigeration meant that beer could be stored or lagered at low temperatures and could be drunk, refreshing and cool, all the year round. The British, suffering neither especially cold winters nor hot summers, doggedly went on brewing their beer in the traditional fashion. Naturally, British brewers took advantage of modern methods to improve the quality and keeping properties of their products. But it was not until the late 20th century that lager beer made any inroads into the British market and its arrival had more to do with pump-priming advertising than with consumer demand. While lager now accounts for some four out of every ten pints drunk in Britain, most of our beer, stout, mild, bitter, old ale and barley wine, continues to be brewed in the centuries-old way known as top fermentation.

Iron Age Celts in Britain drank a kind of ale called *curmi*. That first rough and ready ale could have been made by accident: corn, wheat or barley grains were crushed and made into a dough for bread, the dough was left to stand while wet and it fermented spontaneously with wild yeasts in the air. The origins of beer in Egypt and Mesopotamia are better documented. If that seems an unlikely region to give birth to beer, considering both its current climate and strong cultural and religious antipathy to alcohol, it must be remembered that North Africa and the Middle East in the third millenium BC, between 3000 and 2000 years BC, were quite different climatically and culturally. The world was warmer and it rained more. Cereals were grown and cultivated for food from about 6000 BC and the ability to malt those cereals and ferment them into alcohol was widespread in Mesopotamia by 3000 BC. Barley was the most popular grain and nearly half of all cereal production was

Suck it and see: drinking beer through straws in the Middle East between 3000 and 2000BC.

devoted to brewing. According to the Greeks, Bacchus was so affronted by the bibulous behaviour of the people that he stormed out of Babylonia in disgust. But Bacchus was the god of wine and he may have been an early example of a wine snob who regarded beer as an inferior beverage.

As the Egyptians and Babylonians showed by the technical expertise they brought to brewing, beer making is a far more demanding skill than wine making. Wine at its simplest means crushing grapes and allowing the natural yeast on the skin to ferment the sweet juice. If you crush barley nothing happens. The starches in the barley have first to be converted by malting into a soluble fermentable material. While the first beer was almost certainly brewed by accident, its pleasures were quickly appreciated and brewers became recognised craftsmen, distinct from bakers. The Ancient Egyptian hieroglyph for a brewer was *fty* and showed a man straining a cereal mash into a pot through a type of sieve. In Mesopotamia the tradition was to drink beer through straws from a communal pot to stop the husks of the malted barley getting into the drinkers' mouths. The Babylonians clearly did not strain their mash as the Egyptians did, but they were more advanced in other ways. They heated their malts at different temperatures to produce light and dark drinks, rather as modern brewers kiln their malts for shorter or longer periods depending on whether they are producing lager, bitter, mild or stout.

According to legend the Egyptians were taught to brew by the God Osiris. His worldly disciples developed a sizeable industry. Barley was threshed, germinated and malted, made into 'bread cakes' and then soaked, pounded into a thick porridge, strained into a large pot and fermented. Fermentation was encouraged by yeasty deposits in the cracks of the pots and by using the dregs from previous brews. We can only speculate about the taste of that early beer. It was probably both strong and sweet but plants were often added to take the edge off the sweetness. Until the universal adoption of the hop, early brewers sought to use some form of bittering agent to make their brews less cloyingly sweet.

The Egyptians drank their beer as soon as fermentation was complete. The better-off were prepared to pay more for mature zythum, as the fermented drink was called. It was kept in sealed pots until it was clear and more potable. The size of the Ancient Egyptian brewing industry was considerable. The Pharoah Rameses gave 10,000 hectolitres of zythum to the temple priests every year. This flourishing business was stamped out when the Arabs conquered the land in the 8th century AD. They arrived sword in one hand and Koran in the other and ruled that the sale and consumption of alcohol was a sin.

Barley and other cereals reached Northern Europe with the sea-going Phoenicians. As the world's climate changed, a boundary was drawn across Europe, dividing the grape from the grain. In the Mediterranean lands, wine was the staple drink, while the tribes of the north in Germany, Britain and Scandinavia, largely deprived of hot sun and vines, brewed from cereals. In Britain beer was at first confined to the south. Mead and cider were the national drinks, quick and simple to make. The Romans, marching inexorably across Europe, encountered beer in Germany. Tacitus reported that the tribes there drank a liquor brewed from barley or wheat. Pliny wrote that 'The nations of the west have their own intoxicant from grain soaked in water; there are many ways of making it in Gaul and Spain and under different names, though the principle is the same. The Spanish have taught us that these liquors keep well.' The keeping qualities of ale were aided by coopering. The Romans and Greeks still kept their wine in pots but the peoples of the north, including the Celts, had developed the skill of making casks from curved staves of wood for storing both wet and dry goods. In 21 AD Strabo recorded seeing 'wooden pithoi' (vats) in Northern Europe. 'The Celts are fine coopers,' he wrote, 'for their casks are larger than houses.' There was less enthusiasm, though, for the beverage inside the casks. The Emperor Julian was so horrified by the taste of British ale that he was forced to put pen to paper:

On Wine Made from Barley
Who made you and from what?
By the true Bacchus I know you not.
He smells of nectar
But you smell of goat.

Ale no doubt did taste vile to the refined tastes of a Roman emperor. But it was a vital element in the diet of the peoples of Britain and all of Northern Europe and Scandinavia. These were harsh times and the diet of the average inhabitant of the British Isles must have been appalling. Typhoid and cholera abounded. Water was foul and polluted and was safe to drink only when boiled and made sterile during the process of brewing. Bread and beer, both rich in vitamin B, were crucial parts of the early British diet and helped keep at bay some of the more scrofulous diseases. Beer was drunk by men, women and children. When the first strong brew was finished, the grains would be mashed again to produce a weaker 'small' beer. Small beer survived for centuries. It was used for everyday drinking and was enjoyed at breakfast by all members of the family.

So far I have used the words 'beer' and 'ale' indiscriminately. It is time to be more accurate. The words may be synonymous today but their roots are different. Historically ale was a strong, sweetish brew, while beer was a lighter drink made bitter by the use of hops. Hops did not reach Britain until the 15th century. Like the Ancient Egyptians, brewers in Britain used plants to take the sweetness off their ale. The plants included bog myrtle, rosemary and yarrow. The Germans added a mixture of plants known as *gruit* to their ales, a habit that may have influenced the early distillers of gin in the Low Countries.

When the Romans left Britain, taking their wine casks and viniculture with them, the Danes and Saxons came roistering after them. They brought an enormous appetite for *öl*. *Öl* or *ealu* became the national drink. The Anglo-Saxon religion was heavy with ale drinking. Paradise was a great hall where the dead passed their time quaffing ale. In the real world ale or malt were used to pay fines, tolls, rents and debts. All brewing was done in the home and it was the responsibility of the woman or 'ale wife' to ensure that the men were well supplied. Alreck, King of Hordoland, chose Geirhild to be his queen because she brewed good ale. From this period come the expression *wassail* (a boozy celebration) and the habit of marking drinking goblets with pegs to see who could drink the most ale (hence, 'taking a man down a peg or two'). Another Saxon word for ale was *woet*, which survives to this day in the brewing industry as *wort*. It is the name given to the sweet liquid produced by mixing the malt grist with hot water before fermentation.

A 16th-century ale wife or brewster named Elynoure Rummynge. Her visage was hideous but her 'noppy ale' was said to be superb.

The importance of ale drinking at meals, celebrations – and every meal seems to have been a celebration – and funerals meant that the demand often outstripped the supply. Some households began to specialise in brewing, no doubt because their ale was considered to be the best. People sought their ale. When a new brew was ready, the ale wife or her husband would place a pole above the door and tie a branch or part of a bush to it. The ale house had arrived. By the time of the Norman invasion ale drinking was so deeply ingrained in the common people that wine was confined to the French rulers and their hangers-on. The Domesday Book records 43 *cerevisiarii* (brewers) and shows that the quality of ale was taken sufficiently seriously to impose fines on those who did not brew to an acceptable standard. In Chester, for example, brewers of inferior ales were ducked in the pond or fined four shillings for making bad ale – '*malam cerevisiam faciens.*' The reputation of English ale had improved considerably since the Emperor Julian had dismissed it so woundingly. In 1158 Thomas à Becket took two chariot loads of casks of ale with him on a diplomatic mission to France 'decocted from choice fat grain as a gift for the French who wondered at such an invention – a drink most wholesome, clear of all dregs, rivalling wine in colour and surpassing it in savour.'

The support for ale from a leading member of the priesthood marks another major departure in the history of brewing in Britain. The spread of Christianity had dampened some of the wilder excesses of Anglo-Saxon times. The church not only attempted to regulate drinking but also to corner the market in its production. Monasteries offered accommodation to travellers and set up their own brewhouses to supply them with ale. The bishops looked down on common ale houses and taverns. Ecbright, Archbishop of York, instructed his bishops and priests in the 8th century to provide their own hospices for pilgrims and travellers and to supply them with home-produced ale and food. He forbade his priests to visit ale houses but frequent complaints about over-indulgence by clerics suggests that they made much of their own products. The normal ration of beer, approved by the bishop, in a monastery was a gallon a day of small beer for each monk. Production was prodigious. The malthouse at Fountains Abbey in Yorkshire was sixty square feet and the brewery produced sixty barrels of strong ale every ten days. Monastic ale was fermented inside large wooden casks, a system that survives today in the 'union rooms' of Burton-on-Trent. The strength of the brews was marked on the casks with crosses, the stronger the ale the greater the number of crosses. Given the ecclesiastical surroundings, the crosses may also have been a blessing from the monks, religiously hoping that the brew would not be sour. Ninth-century documents show that monasteries and their breweries reflected the growing stratification of society. The monks brewed the strongest and finest ale, *prima melior*, for distinguished visitors, a second brew, *secunda*, for lay brothers and employees, and a weak *tertia* for the hordes of pilgrims in search of bed and sustenance. The method of producing ale, which survived for many centuries, was to use just one mash for the entire output: the first mash would produce a strong ale, the second a common ale and the final one a small or weak ale considered suitable for women, children and impoverished pilgrims.

Domestic brewing was also growing apace. It was not just in the homes of the common people, where the ale wife or brewster produced ale as part of the daily ritual, but also in the mansions of the nobility. The Normans were assimilated and while they still enjoyed their imported wine had also taken to ale drinking. In 1512 the Northumberland Household Book showed that the aristocratic Percy family consumed the following for breakfast during Lent: a quart of ale each for 'my lord and lady', two pints for 'my lady's gentlewomen' and one and a half gallons for the gentlemen of the chapel and children. There is no reason to doubt that similar amounts were consumed in earlier centuries. There were no other beverages, apart from wine and spirits, to drink. Tea and coffee were unheard of and water was still lethal. Before our forebears are dismissed as hopeless drunks, it must be borne in mind that the heating of houses was rudimentary,

13

people wore several layers of warm clothes for most of the year and they would quickly have burnt off the effects of alcohol.

The brewery of Queen's College in Oxford was founded in 1340 and survived until 1939. Except for the use of a thermometer, the brewery remained unchanged and gives a fascinating glimpse of a medieval brewery used both in monasteries and large houses. The mash tun was made of memel oak and had two outlet pipes covered with metal strainers to contain the grain. The modern method of spraying or 'sparging' the spent grains with hot water to extract the maximum amount of sugar was unknown. The wort was run into an underback below the mash tun and was then pumped by hand to an open copper, where it was boiled. The wort was cooled in large vessels that held 216 gallons and run into a fermenting round and pitched with yeast. As soon as a vigorous fermentation started, the ale was transferred to casks in the cellar where the yeast frothed out of the casks into a trough. Once fermentation was complete, the casks were sealed and the ale left to mature. The ale was twice as strong as an average modern beer and a double strength Chancellor's Ale was also brewed from time to time.

In medieval times, the first attempts were made to curb drinking through taxation or legislation. The earliest efforts were as unsuccessful as more recent ones. In the 13th century a common law was enacted that levied a tax known as a scot on ale consumed in ale houses. But common law held good only on open or cultivated land. Most of Britain was then covered with thick woodland and drinkers anxious to enjoy their ale free of the taxmen took off to the woods where secret ale houses were set up. The woodland revels were known as 'scot ales' after the tax. Drinkers who avoided paying the tax got away 'scot free'. In 1267 Henry III, anxious to protect the quality of the people's basic foods, introduced the Assize of Bread and Ale. The quality of the ingredients was strictly controlled and prices for strong and small ale were laid down. To stop drinkers getting short measure in ale houses and taverns, pots were only allowed to be sold if they carried an official seal. The assize was followed by a vigorous Tumbril and Pillory Statute that fined brewers and bakers who infringed the law. Repeated infringements received more serious punishment: 'If the offence be grievous and often and will not be corrected, then he or she shall suffer corporal punishment, to wit the baker to the Pillory, the brewster to the Tumbril or Flogging.'

The luckless brewster or ale wife was clearly held in poor regard. In one of the Chester Miracle Plays of the 14th century, Christ redeems all the characters from the fires of Hell save for the brewster, who admits:

> Some time I was a taverner
> A gentle gossip and a tapster
> Of wine and ale a trusty brewer
> Which woe hath me bewrought.
> Of cans I kept no true measure,
> My cups I sold at my pleasure,
> Deceiving many a creature,
> Tho' my ale were nought.

She is carried off by demons and flung back into the mouth of Hell, still holding her short measure pot. A carving of an ale wife being thrown into Hell can be seen in Ludlow Church, indicating that short measure was a problem not confined to Chester.

The authorities were determined to enforce the strictures of the Assize of Bread and Ale. They created the post of ale conner, a sort of early version of the excise officer whose task was to visit every public brewery and taste each brew. The ale was rejected if it was not of suitable strength. An absurd but delightful legend grew up around the post of ale conner. Many books claim that to test the strength of a new brew he would pour some on to a bench and then sit in the puddle. After a certain time he would rise. If his leather breeches stuck to the bench then the ale was of the required strength. It is more likely that the conner preferred to taste the brews rather than sit in them, as the *Cobbler of Canterbury* suggests:

> A nose he had that gan show,
> What liquor he loved I trow;
> For he had before long seven yeare
> Been of the towne the ale conner.

Legislation began to refashion brewing, weeding out the bad from the good. But now a great upheaval was to arrive in the shape of the hop plant, an upheaval that would divide drinker against drinker and ultimately lay the grounds for the rise of the great commercial brewers.

On the trail of
the loathsome bine

The arrival of the hop plant and the debate that raged for centuries over the merits of sweet ale and hopped beer.

That 'vile, pernicious weed' the hop plant.

The hop made its first brief appearance in Britain in Roman times. It was brought by the invaders not as an addition to local ale but as a food. The Romans considered the hop to be a delicacy like asparagus. As they tended not to invite members of the indigenous population to dine it is safe to assume that the British were unaware of the hop's existence. They were to stay in this state of cheerful ignorance for several centuries. On the continent of Europe, however, hops were used in the brewing process from the 8th century AD and possibly earlier. The hop, *humulus lupulus*, is a hardy perennial plant and a member of the same family as both cannabis and the nettle. It was grown in Babylon around 200 AD and knowledge of the hop, the ability to grow it and an awareness of its importance in brewing were carried into the Caucasus and later into parts of Germany by the Slavs during the great migrations of people that followed the break up of the Roman empire. Hop gardens existed in the Hallertau region of Germany in 736 AD: it is still one of the greatest hop growing areas of Europe. In 1079 the Abbess Hildegarde of St Ruprechtsberg near Bingen referred to the use of hops in beer. Hop cultivation was also reported in Prague, already emerging as an important brewing centre.

Just as in Britain at a later period, the hop was at first fiercely resisted. Gruit, a mixture of other plants, continued to be used in Germany and other areas until the 16th century. In Russia Archduke Vassili II forbade the use of hops. In Cologne, the Archbishop cornered the gruit market through the Grutrecht and attempted to outlaw the hop. But the hop is a tough little plant to put down and its use spread. Drinkers appreciated the taste of hopped beer and the brewers grasped its importance as not just a bittering agent but as a preservative that prolonged the life of their brews. This quality was of particular importance in countries with climates that made brewing impossible during the hot summer months. Beers brewed in the spring had to have remarkable keeping qualities to last until the autumn and the hop had a vital role to play. Inside the head of the hop are oils and resins, including alpha acid, which give the characteristic aroma or 'hoppy nose' of a beer and which also help to prevent bacterial infection.

By the 14th century the Dutch had acquired a taste for the strongly hopped beers of Hamburg. As in Germany the gruit producers tried without success to hold back the hop but its influence and its growth spread. By 1400 the Dutch merchants who came to trade in Kent and Sussex introduced both hopped beer and hop cultivation into the Winchelsea area. They could not stomach the heavy, sweet ale of the English and imported beer from the Low Countries. Hops made slow progress. Patriotic English drinkers muttered darkly about 'strangers' and 'bere bruers' and no doubt nodded sagely when two such 'bruers', Thomas Seyntleger and John Goryng, were involved in a court case in London in 1473. The Brewers' Company was set up in 1437 expressly to defend the interests of ale producers. The company requested that 'no hops, herbs or other like thing be put into any ale or liquor whereof ale shall be made – but only liquor, malt and yeast' (liquor was and remains the brewer's name for water). But the hop had put down its roots. In 1503 Richard Arnold in his book *Customs of London* gave a recipe for brewing as follows: 'To brewe beer; 10 quarters malt, 2 quarters wheat, 2 quarters oats, 40lbs hops. To make 60 barrels of single beer.' Not only was the hop accepted by Arnold but so was the word beer. However his book also calls for stringent laws to forbid 'Flemings and Dutchmen' from brewing in England. His xenophobia was mild compared to others. The use of hops was forbidden in Norwich, a city where many Flemish weavers settled. In 1519 the use of the 'wicked and pernicious weed, hops' was prohibited in Shrewsbury. Henry VIII, a man who liked his ale, instructed his court brewer not to use hops or brimstone: the monarch was right to condemn the latter ingredient.

The hop's onward march was boosted by a large influx of Flemish weavers into south-east England in 1524. A piece of doggerel at the time complained that

> Hops, Reformation, Bays and Beer
> Came to England in one bad year.

An indication of the support for hopped beer can be seen in the powerful little Englander diatribe of Andrew Boorde in his *Compendyous Regyment or Dyetary of Health* written in 1542: 'Beer is made of malte, hoppes and water; it is the natural drynke for a Dutcheman, and nowe of lete dayes it is much used in England to the detryment of many Englysshe people; specyally it kylleth them the which be troubled with the colyke; and the stone and the strangulion; for the drynke is a colde drynke, yet it doth make a man fat, and doth inflate the bely, as it doth appere by the Dutche men's faces and belyes. If the bere be well served and be fyned and not new, it doth qualify heat of the lyver.' Ale on the other hand 'is made of malte and water; and they the which do put any other thynge to ale than is rehersed, except yest, barme or godesgood, doth sofyticat theyr ale. Ale for an Englysche man is a naturall drinke. Ale must have these propertyes: it must be fresshe and clear, it muste not be ropy or smoky, nor it must have no weft nor tayle. Ale should not be dronke under V days olde.' Boorde was not only wildly and ludicrously wrong about the effects of drinking beer but was less than accurate about the brewing of ale. Yeast and 'godisgood' are one and the same. The latter term was used for centuries by even experienced brewers who could only watch in wonder as yeast went about its energetic and mysterious activities. Rope referred to an infection of the wort and survives today in the expression 'ropy' if you are feeling unwell.

In spite of such tirades, hops were not just being imported but grown in England. The first hop gardens were laid out in Kent in 1520. The county offered ideal conditions. Land enclosure was well established there, offering protection to farmers. The soil

21

was excellent and there was an abundance of wood for making hop poles and for charcoal for drying the hops. Kentish farmers were prosperous and could afford the initial expense of setting up hop gardens, as a rhyme of the time suggests:

A nobleman of Cailes
A Knight of Wales
A Laird of the North Countree,
A Yeoman of Kent with his yearly rent,
Could buy them out all three.

Beer using Kentish hops was soon being brewed in the south of England. It was beer not ale that was sent to France in 1522 to refresh the English troops stationed there. Army accounts for 1542 record the cost of buying the new ingredient in brewing: '10,042 pounds of hops at 10 shillings per hundred.' Beer was also drunk on state occasions along with ale. At a royal banquet in Windsor Park in 1528 fifteen gallons of beer and fifteen gallons of ale were ordered for the guests. The beer cost 20d, the ale 2s 6d. The difference in price is significant. The better keeping qualities of hopped beer meant that less malt had to be used. Ale was traditionally brewed to a high gravity or strength to prolong its life. In *A Perfite Platforme for a Hoppe Garden*, first published in 1574, Reynold Scot set down the advantages of hopped beer: 'Whereas you cannot make above 8–9 gallons of indifferent ale from 1 bushel of malt, you may draw 18–20 gallons of very good beer. If your ale may endure a fortnight, your beer through the benefit of the hop, shall continue a month, and what grace it yieldeth to the taste, all men may judge that have sense in their mouths. And if controversy be betwixt Beer and Ale, which of them shall have the place of pre-eminence, it sufficeth for the glory and commendation of the Beer that, here in our own country, ale giveth place unto it and that most part of our countrymen do abhor and abandon ale as a loathsome drink.' Scot's book, which ran to three editions, is one of the most important in the history of the brewing industry. He was educated at Oxford University and farmed in Kent. With the aid of woodcuts he described in fine detail the way to prepare the soil

Engraving from Reynold Scott's
A Perfitte Platforme for a Hoppe Garden.

and to erect poles as soon as the hops appeared above the ground. Left to their own devices hops will run wild, trailing along the ground or in hedges. As continental growers had found, it was essential to train the stems or *bines* of the hops upwards to ensure sound growth, maximum exposure to sun and light and ease of picking. Scot advised on the best way to pick hops – 'cut them assunder with a sharpe hooke and with a forked staffe take them from the poles' – and designed an oast house where hops are dried and stored.

The profitable advantages of hopped beer were not lost on the brewers. Brewing was still carried on in homes large and small but towns were crammed with ale houses (a census of 1577 showed there were 19,759 public drinking places in England and Wales and 88 per cent were ale houses. The population was 3,700,000, which meant there was a retail drinking outlet for every 187 people). The owners of the larger and more successful outlets quickly latched on to the fact that they could not only satisfy the demand for the new hopped beer but enrich themselves at the same time. It was the advent of hopped beer that saw the rise of successful brewers who moved on from the limitations of their own ale houses to set up in business and brew on a commercial basis. In his *Quip for an Upstart Courier* in 1592 Robert Greene poured scorn on the new breed: 'And you, masser Brewer, that growe to be worth forty thousand pounds by your selling of soden water, what subtility have you in making your beare to spare the malt and put in more of the hop to make you drinke (be barly never so cheape) not a whit the stronger, yet never sel a whit the more measure for mony; you can, when you have taken all the hart of the malt away, then clap on store of water ('tis cheape enough) and mash a tunning of small beare, that it scoures a man's maw like Rhenish wine; in your conscience how many barrels draw you out of a quarter of malt? Fie, fie, I conceal your falsehood, lest I should be too broad in setting down your faults.' Greene was mourning the passing of an era. Commercial or common brewers would not be deterred by his irony. By the middle of the 16th century there were 26 common brewers in London, most of them based in Southwark, conveniently close to the hop market at the Borough. At the same time, two Acts were passed in 1552 and 1553 to licence ale houses, inns and taverns. An ale house was licensed to sell just beer or ale. An inn provided food and accommodation as well while the tavern, a superior institution, was able to sell wine and spirits. The hop had transformed British ale. Now the stage was set for the creation of a commercial brewing industry that would see the demise of the domestic brewer and the rise of the 'tied house'.

CHAPTER THREE

From Gin Lane to Porters' Pleasure

Beer's image is boosted by the terrible devastation caused by the mass consumption of bootleg gin. The development of a strong dark beer in London known as 'entire butt' or more popularly porter boosts the rise of the great commercial brewers.

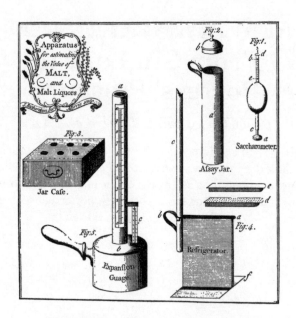

*Hydrometer or saccharometer circa 1784
which enabled brewers to accurately
measure the gravity of their beers.*

The image of beer as a wholesome and healthy drink was given a fillip in the 17th and 18th centuries when gin arrived in Britain. The appalling depravity caused by the widespread consumption of gut-rot gin encouraged the governments of the day to elevate the importance of beer drinking in controlled premises. It was not the intention of Franciscus de la Boë, the professor of medicine at Leiden University in the Netherlands in the early 17th century, to poison the British populace. He invented gin with medicinal reasons in mind, as a cure for soldiers suffering from fevers picked up in the East Indies. His *essence de Genièvre* was a distillation of barley and rye that was redistilled with juniper berries and other flavourings. Juniper, he claimed, soothed the kidneys. English troops fighting in Flanders under the command of Sir Philip Sidney acquired a taste for 'geneva' and drank large draughts of it before going into battle, an activity that gave rise to the expression 'Dutch courage'. As John Masefield's poem *The Everlasting Mercy* suggests, 'geneva' did more harm than good to the drinker's internal organs:

> Meanwhile my friend, 'twould be no sin
> To mix more water with your gin
> We're neither saints nor Philip Sidneys
> But mortal men with mortal kidneys

The soldiers returned to England with a taste for 'Hollands' or 'geneva' but French brandy was a more popular spirit among the people. Charles I granted a charter to the Worshipful Company of Distillers and home-produced gin rivalled the Dutch variety in its quality. The position changed dramatically when England and France went to war in 1688, James II fled to France and the throne was handed to a Dutchman, William of Orange. Imports of French brandy were banned and gin became the popular drink. Some agricultural workers were given gin as part of their wages. Queen Anne, who succeeded William, revoked the privileges of the Distillers Company to roars of bucolic approval from a parliament packed with farmers and landlords. They could not export corn to France and were anxious to sell it to unlicensed distillers at home. The result was a tragic period in British history. Gin was sold by barbers and tobacconists. It was available on market stalls and was hawked door to door. Such unpalatable additives as turpentine and sulphuric acid further adulterated the vile concoctions produced by a vast army of home distillers. In 1729 the Middlesex magistrates estimated that there were 7,044 regular 'dram shops' in London, which meant that one house in four sold gin. A writer at the time commented: 'One half of the town seems set up to furnish poison to the other half.'

Gin shops sold their product at 1d a pint. Children were seen drunk in the streets. People died in vast numbers from 'gin drinker's liver' – atrophic cirrhosis of the liver. The morbid sign outside one gin shop in Southwark – 'Drunk for 1d, dead drunk for 2d, clean straw for nothing' – summed up the state of misery that prevailed in London and other cities. In London there were twice as many burials as baptisms. A report in 1736 described a building in Smithfield where gin was sold. It had a room at the back where drunks were 'laid together in heaps promiscuously, men, women and children, till they recover their senses, when they proceed to drink on, or, having spent all they had, go out to find wherewithal to return to the same drunken pursuit; and how they acquire more money the sessions paper [court reports] too often acquaint us.' Between 1684 and 1740 gin production rose from half a million gallons a year to 20 million. Duty was 2d a gallon and most distillers openly thumbed their noses at the excise men, who could not cope with the untrammelled production. Hogarth's savage portrait 'Gin Lane' in 1751 stressed the terrible dissolution of the time. Houses are falling apart, a corpse is being put into a cart and a woman in the foreground is so drunk that she is dropping her small child over a railing. The pawnbroker and the undertaker watch the scene with undisguised pleasure. The caption to the frightening scene declares:

> Gin! curs'd fiend with fury fraught,
> Makes human race a prey,
> It enters by a deadly draught,
> And steals our life away.

Hogarth's picture of 'Beer Street' is absurdly romantic, with healthy, robust people and well-preserved buildings. Only the pawnbroker is miserable. The inscription

> Beer! happy produce of our isle,
> Can sinewy strength impart,
> And wearied with fatigue and toil,
> Can cheer each manly heart.

was a gross over-simplification of the real life of the urban poor. But there is no doubt that those who stuck to beer and ignored gin enjoyed healthier if not wealthier lives. The Gin Act of 1736, with heavy taxation on production, had served only to make matters worse. Hawkers, peddlers and quack chemists sold rough gin in coloured bottles under such fanciful names as Blue Ruin, Daffy's Elixir, My Lady's Eye-Water and Parliamentary Brandy. Gin consumption rose. A new Act of 1742 clamped down on the retailers not the producers. A licensing system made it illegal for retailers to distil their own gin. A decade later, Hogarth showed that gin drinking was still widespread and ruinous but the problem eased as better quality gin was introduced by such new commercial manufacturers as Gilbey, Booth and Gordon, and ornate 'gin palaces' provided pleasanter licensed places in which to enjoy it.

Beer had profited from gin's disreputable image. The authorities promoted it as a decent, sensible tipple. Beer had survived the twin upheavals of the dissolution of the monasteries under Henry VIII and the Civil War. Cromwell's republic had frowned upon beer drinking and introduced excise duty on it but consumption was unchecked. The monarchy was restored but the old order had gone for ever. The manufacturing and trading

29

classes were in the ascendancy and science and technology were no longer looked upon as creations of the devil. There was a rapid development of the coal industry and the larger brewers made use of coal to fire their coppers and heat their water. The malting of barley became more proficient. Commercial brewers were making their presence felt and were supplying more than just their own ale houses. Samuel Pepys had a taste for Bide's ale. Alderman John Bide was a man of substance, the Sheriff of London in 1647. In 1667 Pepys confided in his diary: 'Thence home and went as far as Mile End with Sir W. Pen, whose coach took him up there for his country-house; and after having drunk there, at the Rose and Crowne, a good house for Alderman Bide's ale, we parted.' A few days' later he was back in Mile End with his wife 'and there drank Bide's ale, and so home.' A week later he again records that he journeyed to Mile End to enjoy the good alderman's ale. Pepys was an early example of that determined breed of English drinkers who will undertake long and often perilous journeys to find the finest ale.

In Thomas Tryon's book *A New Art of Brewing Beer, Ale and Other Sorts of Liquor*, published in 1691, he remarked that 'brewing is become a trade.' By the end of the century 'brewing victuallers' who produced only for their own premises were in decline in London though they continued to dominate the rural market. In London in 1699 there were 194 common brewers who produced 962,440 barrels of strong beer and ale and 690,640 of small or weak beer. The excise officers logged only 6,000 barrels of strong beer and 6,700 barrels of small from brewing victuallers. London was not typical of the British Isles. The country was still mainly rural and both hops and improvements in brewing skills were slow to spread. But the capital set the pace. How London brewed today, the rest of Britain would brew tomorrow.

The distinction between ale and beer was becoming blurred. While John Taylor in his laboriously titled book *Ale Ale-vated into the Ale-titude* could still berate beer in 1651 as 'a Dutch boorish liquor . . . a saucy intruder in this Land' the attitude had changed substantially by 1695 when James Lightbody produced his important work *Every Man his Own Gauger*. (*Gauger* was the term used for an excise man or collector of taxes on brewing.) In his advice on brewing he suggests that 'the quantity of hops you are to use for Ale is 3 pound to 8 Bushels of Malt; if it be Beer, you put 6 pound to 8 bush.' Lightbody was also the first known writer to recommend the use of isinglass to clear beer of its yeasty deposit. Isinglass is made from the bladder of the sturgeon fish and its use at the turn of the century suggests that drinkers were becoming more fussy and wanted beer that was clear and clean to the taste. There was now no shortage of advice on how to brew better beer. In 1727 *A Guide to Gentleman Farmers and Housekeepers for Brewing the Finest Malt Liquors* and the *Dictionnaire Oeconomique* or *Family Dictionary*, both believed to be the work of Professor R. Bradley of the University of Cambridge, went into great detail on such matters as temperatures for mashing and boiling, and handling of yeast, the ratio of malt to hops and the best water and coke to use. Bradley considered the finest brewing water in England to be that 'at Castleton in Derbyshire, commonly called the Devil's Arse, which oozes from a great rock – ale made from Castleton water has been found to be clear in three days after it was barrelled as the spring water itself.' Bradley gave recipes for brewing strong March and October beers, with 11 bushels of malt to a 54 gallon hogshead cask, and six or seven bushels for ordinary brews. For 'ordinary' read strong by today's standards. Although there were no scientific ways of measuring the strength of beer, modern experts consider that strong beers of the 18th century had an 'original gravity' of 1080–1100 degrees, ferociously strong by today's standards – 1100 degrees is roughly equal to 11 per cent alcohol, the strength of an average modern wine. Middle range beers of the time had a gravity of 1050 degrees, similar to one of the very strongest draught bitters brewed in modern Britain, Fuller's Extra Special Bitter from Chiswick in London. Only small beer, with a gravity of 1025 degrees, would be considered weak today, but that small beer was drunk by

Ralph Thrale took over Halsey's brewery – later to become Courage – in 1729. Charrington opened in 1776 and Mr Ind, then without Coope, set up in business in Romford in 1779. The two Williams, Worthington and Bass, were creating their humble enterprises in Burton-on-Trent and another William, Younger, was preparing to please the palates of drinkers in the east of Scotland. Across the Irish sea, a brewer named Arthur Guinness leased a rundown brewery in St James's Gate in Dublin in 1759. None of these newcomers to brewing could be dismissed as common victuallers or ale house brewers. They were entrepreneurs for whom brewing was their sole occupation. And the London brewers and later Arthur Guinness were to make their fortunes from a new beer for which there was such a voracious demand that only establishments with large brewing capacities could cope. The beer was called porter.

Porter was a dark beer, almost black in colour. It looked and may even have tasted rather like modern Guinness stout, though it was considerably stronger. London water, rich in calcium carbonate, was ideally suited to producing dark beer. Porter, heavily hopped, had such prodigious keeping qualities that it could be brewed all the year round. It had to be matured for several months, which meant that large amounts of capital were tied up in its production. Porter, in short, was the beer that produced a modern, commercial brewing industry and sounded the death knell for the small ale house brewer who produced beer when the occasion demanded and never in warm weather. Porter was invented according to legend by Ralph Harwood, owner of the Bell Brewhouse in Shoreditch, in 1722. A popular beer of the time was a mixture of pale, young brown ale and 'stale' (mature) brown ale. It was known as 'three threads' – probably a corruption of 'three thirds' – and was a nuisance for busy landlords and potmen because they had to make frequent journeys to the ale house cellar to draw the mixture from three casks. Harwood, sensible fellow, thought it would simplify life if he brewed one beer with the same taste as 'three threads'. It was called 'entire butt' because it came from just one cask or butt and the name was quickly shortened to just 'entire'. The beer became so popular with the street market porters in the area that entire was replaced by a new name – porter. It quickly made its mark. In 1726 a visiting Frenchman, Cesar de Saussure, reported home: 'Would you believe it, although water is to be had in abundance in London and of fairly good quality, absolutely none is drunk? The lower classes, even the paupers, do not know what it is to quench their thirst with water. In this country nothing but beer is drunk and it is made in several qualities. Small beer is what everyone drinks when thirsty; it is used even in the best houses and costs only a penny a pot. Another kind of beer is called porter . . . because the greater quantity of this beer is consumed by the working classes. It is a thick and strong beverage, and the effect it produces if drunk in excess, is the same as that of wine; this porter costs 3d the pot. In London there are a number of houses where nothing but this sort of beer is sold . . . It is said more grain is consumed in England for making beer than making bread.' The Old Blue Last in Great Eastern Street, London EC2, now a Truman tied house, claims that it was the first outlet for porter. By 1758 H. Jackson wrote in his *Essay on Bread* that 'Beer, commonly call'd Porter, is almost become the universal Cordial of the Populace.'

The demand for porter was so vast that some of the new commercial brewers did not bother with pale or amber beers. There was a great deal of money to be made from porter brewing. In 1763 the *Gentleman's Magazine* remarked caustically on pleas of overwork from the new entrepreneurs: 'Brewers pining at the hardships they labour under and rolling away in their coaches and six to their several villas to drown their grief in burgundy and champagne.' Samuel Whitbread was a case in point. He came from Bedfordshire, the son of a farmer. When his mother was widowed she sent Samuel, the seventh of eight children, to London to be apprenticed to a brewer, John Wightman, for a substantial fee of £300. Young Samuel learnt his trade well and in 1742 opened his own small brewery at Old Street. His daughter recalled those hard times when she wrote:

'In the early part of his trade, he sat up 4 nights a week by his brewing copper, refreshed himself by washing plentifully with cold water and a clean shirt, and when the state of the Barley permitted his quitting, retired for 2 hours to his closet reading the Scriptures and devotional exercises.' He was the very model of a modern master brewer. Business thrived and in 1745 Whitbread moved, lock, stock and barrels, to a new brewery in Chiswell Street. Pale and amber beers continued for some time to be brewed at Old Street. Chiswell Street was a porter brewery and built on a scale never before seen in Britain. By 1760 Whitbread had built a porter tun room 'the unsupported roof span of which is exceeded in its majestic size only by that of Westminster Hall'. (The building stands today but is used by Whitbread as offices.) The porter was matured in enormous underground cisterns, each containing 4,000 barrels of beer. In 1785 James Watt installed a 'stupendous' steam engine in the brewery to revolutionise production. It became one of the great sights of London, so much so that in 1787 George III and Queen Charlotte came to wonder at it. The *London Chronicle* reported: 'The time appointed for the visit in Chiswell Street was ten in the morning on Saturday last. Curiosity and courtesy outran the clock. Their Majesties were there a quarter before ten . . . They were received at the door by Mr Whitbread and his daughter; and politely declining the breakfast that was provided, immediately went over the works.'

Samuel Whitbread became the Member of Parliament for Bedford, bought a fine country estate in Hertfordshire, gave generously to charity and had his portrait painted by Sir Joshua Reynolds. It hangs today in Chiswell Street. When he died in 1796 he bequeathed a flourishing business to his son, also called Samuel. In 1812 Chiswell Street brewed 122,000 barrels of porter a year but Whitbread was outstripped by Barclay Perkins (270,000), Meux Reid (188,000) and Truman Hanbury (150,000). Absurd braggadocio surrounded the brewing of porter. When Henry Thrale opened his new porter vat, one hundred people sat down to dine in it. Meux built one that was 60 feet wide and 23

Samuel Whitbread's Chiswell Street brewery.

feet high and 200 guests dined in that one. In 1795 Meux added another vat that was big enough to hold 20,000 barrels. The brewers' determination to each build bigger and bigger vessels was halted by a tragedy in 1814 when a porter vat burst at the Horse Shoe Brewery close to Tottenham Court Road. The deluge swept away brewery walls and other nearby buildings and eight people were killed by 'drowning, injury, poisoning by the porter fumes or drunkenness.'

The rise of the commercial brewers was made possible by new technologies that required capital outlays beyond the dreams and pockets of small ale house victuallers. James Watt's steam engine had revolutionised Chiswell Street and his and other companies installed engines for the other major brewing concerns. In the late 18th and 19th centuries other innovations came thick and fast. The hydrometer or saccharometer made it possible to measure scientifically the specific gravity of wort by determining the amount of sugar present before fermentation. The brewers could produce beers of consistent strength and use their malt more judiciously. The thermometer measured the temperature of worts in the mash tun, the copper and the fermenting vessel. Before Fahrenheit and Boerhaave perfected the thermometer and its application, the temperature of the mash had been determined by the use of the elbow, as a parent tests the heat of a baby's bath water, or by the brewer's ability to see his face reflected in the liquor before it was obscured by steam. Michael Combrune's *Essay on Brewing* and *Theory and Practice of Brewing*, published in 1758 and 1762, outlined a more scientific approach to brewing with the use of the thermometer, though he could not refrain from mentioning that Fahrenheit and Boerhaave were both 'Hollanders': there was still some lingering antipathy to the influence of the Dutch on British brewing. John Richardson's *Philosophical Principles of the Science of Brewing* in 1784 said that 'it is evident how much the Use of the thermometer ought to be studied by the brewer . . . Without this instrument it is impossible he can accommodate his practice to the different qualities of his malts so as to secure to himself every obtainable advantage.' Cast-iron mash tuns replaced wood and steam power drove rakes to stir the mash. The introduction of sparging from around the middle of the 19th century meant that sugar could be extracted more efficiently from the wort. Instead of producing strong, medium and small beer from the same mash, the commercial brewers began to restrict each brew to its own mash. The sparging device, driven by steam, circled over the mash tun as the wort was drawn out and sprinkled the grains with more hot liquor. Copper tubes were placed inside brewing vessels to heat water while refrigeration, one of the most fundamentally important inventions of the 19th century, made it possible to cool the hopped wort quickly before fermentation and then allow the new, rough beer to condition and mature in cooled tanks. With refrigeration came the opportunity, seized by the commercial brewers, to produce all the year round. They no longer shut up shop in the summer or produced exceptionally strong beers to last through the warmer months. Beer of consistent quality and strength was brewed from January to December.

For centuries brewing had been dogged by the misfortune of infection during fermentation. In 1680 Leeuwenhoek, another man from the Low Countries, had described the working of yeast cells and Lavoisier in the 18th century showed how the action of yeast on the sweet wort produced alcohol and carbon dioxide. Then came Louis Pasteur with his research into yeast strains and infections. He visited several British breweries, including Whitbread's and Younger's in Edinburgh. At Chiswell Street he drew the brewer's attention to micro-organisms in the sediment of some spoiled beer and explained how these bacilli infected the fermenting beer and made it go sour. Whitbread and other companies in quick succession acquired microscopes, kept their breweries scrupulously clean and developed pure yeast strains that were stored in refrigerators to avoid infection.

The commercial brewers had to sell their products and were no longer satisfied with a system in which customers would arrive at the brewery with their own pots and vessels for a 'carry out'. The brewers began to buy up ale houses and establish their

Louis Pasteur at work in his laboratory.

own retail outlets or 'tied houses'. The advocates of free trade in
the early 19th century saw the brewery tied house as an
infringement of liberty. They joined forces with the farming
lobby, who were concerned by the rising popularity of tea, to
introduce the Beer Act of 1830 which abolished duty on beer and
allowed anyone to sell beer by paying two guineas for a licence.
Sydney Smith had hoped that the act would break the strangle-
hold of the licensing magistrates who were in league with the
commercial brewers: 'One of the most enormous and scandalous
Tyrannies ever exercised upon any people.' Smith and his fellow
free traders had learned little from the effects of unfettered gin
sales a century before. The people went on a drunken rampage.
A few days after the Beer Act became law, Smith was forced to
admit: 'Everybody is drunk. Those who are not singing are
sprawling. The sovereign people are in a beastly state.' Two acts
attempted to improve the situation and the Wine and Beerhouse
Act of 1869 placed all retail outlets under the control of the
justices again. The result was the opposite of the situation the
free traders had sought. Thousands of small publicans went
bankrupt. The big brewers snapped up these new outlets for a
song and further entrenched their position.

A quieter piece of legislation occurred in 1845. Excise duty was abolished on glass. Bottles and glasses could now be produced more cheaply and drinkers could see what they were getting. They didn't always like what they saw. Porter was thick and cloudy. Fussy drinkers demanded clarity and that demand was met not in London but in Burton-on-Trent.

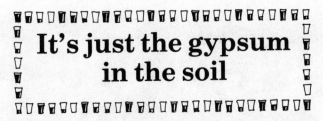

CHAPTER FOUR

It's just the gypsum in the soil

Burton-on-Trent becomes the beer boom town as the light, sparkling ales brewed there are in great demand in the colonies and then outstrip sales of porter at home.

Dixie & Co: coopers at Bass, Burton-on-Trent in the 19th century.

The Earl of Mercia, Wulfric Spot, founded an abbey in Staffordshire in 1002 AD and the monks of Burton Abbey, like their brothers in other isolated rural communities, began to brew ale as an essential part of their diet and as a refreshment for pilgrims. They discovered that the water from the wells in the area produced ale that had a fine taste and excellent keeping qualities. The water was rich in calcium sulphate – gypsum – and other minerals. Brewers of pale, bitter beers today add salts to their water supplies to achieve that unique Burton taste and sparkle; they say that they 'Burtonise' the water. Essentially, Burton water is hard, unlike the softer water of London, better suited to brewing dark beer. The quality of Burton ales spread, even in medieval England. When Mary Queen of Scots was held prisoner in Tutbury Castle close to Burton in the 16th century she had supplies of ale sent to her. She used the empty casks to send messages to her supporters but the loyal brewer passed them to agents of Queen Elizabeth and Mary's go-between, Anthony Babington, went to the scaffold as a result.

By 1600 Burton-on-Trent had 46 licensed victuallers who produced ales for a population of just 1,500. Small supplies of the local brews went to London. Burton ale became something of a cult drink in the Peacock in Gray's Inn Lane and the Dagger Inn in nearby Holborn, inns frequented by the young blades of the time who did not wish to emulate the hoi-polloi with their dark ales. By the early 18th century there are references in London journals to 'Hull ale' but this was almost certainly beer from Burton that had reached the east coast port by way of the Trent. In 1712 Joseph Addison noted in the *Spectator*: 'We concluded our walk with a glass of Burton ale.' The Trent Navigation Act of 1699 had made the river navigable from

Burton to Shardlow and by 1712 provided easy passage to Gains-borough and Hull. Burton beers could now be moved around central and northern England with ease. More importantly, they could be exported. Entrepreneurs in the Burton area were quick to seize on this new opportunity for business. The first of the merchant brewers, Benjamin Printon, opened his brewery early in the 18th century and was followed by half a dozen competitors, including William Worthington. In 1777 a Burton transport businessman named William Bass noted that his carts were taking ever greater supplies of beer from Burton to other towns. He started his own small brewery and ran a dual business, producing beer in the winter and concentrating on his transport firm in the summer. But his beer became popular and eventually he sold the carrying company to a man called Pick-ford. Pickford flourished but his success was overshadowed by William Bass's. He established a brewing firm that was to become the biggest in the world within a century and along with the other Burton brewers was to change the nature of British beer.

By 1780 there were 13 commercial breweries in Burton. Between 40 and 70 per cent of their production went as exports to the Baltic. It is curious to hear modern brewers complain that traditional beer does not 'travel'. Less than 200 years ago similar beer was travelling and being lapped up in countries as diverse and far apart as Russia, India and the islands of the Caribbean. In 1800 Bass had nine agents in St Petersburg, 11 in Riga, 25 in Danzig, one in Elsinore and four each in Hamburg, Bremen and Hanover. London and Dublin were exporting beer, too, and the fame of a few brewers' names at home and abroad prompted the lines from C.S. Calverley:

> O Beer! O Hodgson, Guinness, Allsopp, Bass!
> Names that should be on every infant's tongue!

Those early commercial brews from Burton were sweet and brown, though less dark than the stouts and porters of London. The brewers had yet to unlock the special properties of Burton water. The key was provided by an unlikely benefactor, Napoleon Bonaparte. As his armies swept across Europe, he closed port after port and country after country to British exports. The German and Baltic trade was cut off. The Burton brewers had problems at home without the collapse of their export trade. The price of raw materials had risen and so had labour costs as workers threatened to leave brewing for other manufacturing industries or the armed forces unless they were better paid. Several of the Burton brewers went under. Others were forced to amalgamate as the new name of Bass, Ratcliff and Gretton shows. They had to seek fresh markets, for their style of beer was not then widely popular in London. They found that market in India and in so doing produced a type of beer called India Pale Ale, the forerunner of modern bitter. With the growth of the British Empire in India a vast and largely untapped market existed among the troops, civil servants and businessmen stationed or working there. Curiously, that market was first cornered by the London brewer Hodgson. Against the trend in the capital, he managed to brew a light-coloured beer with a high hop rate that survived the long sea journey to India. Hodgson called his export beer India Ale. It is not clear how he managed to produce a light beer in London at the time, for others, including Barclay, had tried and failed but by the early 1800 he had a virtual monopoly of the India trade. When he fell out with his Indian suppliers in 1822, the Burton brewers, desperate for trade, jumped at the opportunity to export to the great continent. They responded to the advice of a Calcutta merchant that 'the ale adapted for this market should be clear, light, bitter pale ale of a moderate strength.' The Burton brewers found that if they lowered the gravity of their beers and used paler malts and heavy amounts of hops they could, with the aid of their hard water, produce just what the India market demanded. The gravity of those India ales was around 1060 degrees, almost half that of the strong, dark London brews. It was a type of beer able to withstand long sea journeys in casks and bottles and was cool and refreshing when drunk in hot climates. By a different route and different method of fermentation, the Burton brewers were following a similar drive in

Europe towards lighter and more thirst-quenching beers.

The Burton brewers were keen to establish a home market for their new type of beer. Trade was slow to pick up at first but chance gave the product a boost. In 1827 a consignment of Bass India Pale Ale for export was wrecked in the Irish Sea. The salvaged casks were auctioned in Liverpool and the buyers sold the beer far and wide. Pale ale's fame spread. It had found its new market. It even took on and conquered the great porter market of London, aided, as we have seen, by the ending of duty on glass. Drinkers could see their beer in glass tankards and they appreciated the clear, sparkling Burton ales. Porter, which had held sway since the early 1700s, went into a rapid decline. London brewers were not yet able to treat their water to reproduce the hard liquor of Burton and several of them hurried to the Staffordshire town. Charrington, Truman, Mann Crossman and Ind Coope (later to merge with Allsopp) were among the London brewers who set up in Burton to brew India Ale for their burgeoning outlets in the south. By 1887 Charrington was brewing 80,000 barrels a year in Burton. Between 1831 and 1847 production at Bass increased six times. When the firm celebrated its centenary in 1877 it was brewing close to one million barrels a year. Bass employed 2,250 men and boys in three breweries, its coopering works and maltings. It had offices and warehouses throughout Britain and had developed its export trade again. In spite of the disruptions of the Napoleonic Wars, Bass was now popular in France and Manet included two bottles of Bass in his painting *The Bar at the Folies Bergères*. The now familiar Bass Red Triangle can be seen on the labels in the picture. The fame of Bass and the resulting rash of forgeries from British and overseas breweries had prompted the company to register its triangle, originally a shipping mark, under the Trade Marks Registration Act of 1875. A member of the company's staff spent an uncomfortable night on the steps of the registrar's office to make sure the red triangle became the very first registered mark under the act. The diligent employee also took the opportunity to register the Bass Red Diamond and Brown Diamond symbols as trade marks two and three.

The railway made the Burton companies national breweries. Their beer could be carried swiftly to all the major parts of industrial Britain and drank in prime condition. The Birmingham and Derby Junction company was the first railway to reach Burton. It was followed by the Midland, the North Staffs, the London and North Western and the Great Northern. When St Pancras station was built in London, its cellars were designed to hold two hogsheads of Burton beer. The iron way was also used to advantage within the breweries to move beer and raw materials around. Both Bass and Worthington built their own narrow gauge systems. At its peak the Bass internal railway had 16 miles of track, 11 engines and 450 wagons and vans. Awed visitors were carried round the great Bass complex in special carriages. Michael Thomas Bass the second had taken to the railway with enormous enthusiasm. The Liberal MP for Derby, he was a

Hops on a train: brewery railway sidings at Burton.

typical Victorian benefactor. His own fortune was assured and he could afford to be generous to the less fortunate. It was not just altruism that encouraged him to donate to the funds of the first railway trade union, the Amalgamated Society of Railway Servants. A contented workforce would transport his beer better than a disgruntled one. Bass would begin a railway journey by walking up to the engine and shaking hands with the driver. On one occasion, after a journey lasting more than ten hours, Bass went back to the engine to thank the driver. He was horrified to find the same man in charge. Bass threatened to withdraw his beer from the company unless they agreed that no driver should run a train for more than eight hours. The company, mindful of the extent of its business with Bass, immediately agreed to his terms.

The railway was also used to reward Bass employees. From 1875 until the First World War, as many as 17 trains would be used to transport brewery workers to Yarmouth, Blackpool, Scarborough or Liverpool for the day. Each participant was given a brochure to mark the day, complete with a list of all outlets for Bass beers en route. Norfolk farm workers who lost their jobs when the harvest was finished were offered employment in the Bass maltings during the winter months. They were given a single railway ticket to Burton, a special suit known locally as a 'Norkie' and their return ticket when it was time to return home.

An anonymous article in the *Daily News* in 1880, reprinted as a pamphlet, described a visit to Bass in Burton. It gives a graphic picture of the size of an enterprise started little more than a century before on an acre of land. In 1880 the Bass empire occupied 140 acres. It used 267,000 quarters of malt a year, 36,000 hundredweight of hops and paid £300,000 in duty. Weekly wages amounted to £2,500. 'Bass has in use 47,000 butts, 160,000 hogsheads, 140,000 barrels and 200,000 kilderkins; a stock of casks in all, in store and scattered over the country, exceeding half a million.' The writer's description of the brewing process is one of the best on record and shows how all the new techniques had been assimilated. When the wort has been run off through the false bottom of the mash tun 'the malt left is "sparged" by a shower bath of hot water to extract from it the last remains of saccharine-matter'. The wort is then pumped by steam power up to the coppers where hops are added and the wort is boiled. It then has to be cooled before it can be fermented. The writer notes that before refrigeration the temperature was often too high to permit brewing. But now the wort is pumped to refrigerators: 'It is difficult to make these out to be anything else than huge flat boxes; but by climbing up and peeping over the edge, we see a shallow lake, laced by successive long straight coils of copper piping . . . the boiled wort is flowing slowly from the coolers through this mighty submerged snake, while the cold water that covers it has given to it a slow steady motion at right angles to the flow of the wort, so as to intensify the refrigerating power'.

There is still a link with the past. Once fermentation has started, the fermenting wort is transferred from vessels called squares to the great union room, where it continues to ferment inside large wooden casks that are linked together – held in union – by one long pipe. 'What a ball-room would this union-room make if its floor were clear . . . but instead of dancers it holds 2,500 casks, each one containing 160 gallons.' The fermenting beer gushes up from the casks through swan-necked pipes into a tray called a barm trough. The yeast settles into the trough and beer circulates over it for several days until ferment-ation is complete. It was the union room system, based upon the old monastic style of brewing, that gave Burton beers their distinctive light, quaffable character. The only surviving union room today is in the Marston brewery whose splendid Pedigree ale is one of the most subtle and succulent of beers. Burton beers had another rare quality. In 1894 a Dr Mapother told *Licensing News* that 'I have never found that Bass's India draught pale ale, taken in small quantities at meals, disagrees . . . The drink is laxative, while the contrary is to be said of other ales and porters.' This peculiar liberating effect of union room beers was testified to in the late 1970s when Draught Bass, successor to the original India Pale Ale, was still brewed in the unions. A satisfied but puzzled customer wrote to the company: 'I have recently taken to drinking Draught Bass and enjoy it very much, but I have just one question to ask you: How long will I have to keep my toilet roll in the fridge?' Refrigeration had many unsuspected benefits for the modern brewing industry.

The union room at Bass, Burton: fermenting beer rose from the oak casks into the trough above where it circulated over yeast.

CHAPTER FIVE

Russian Imperial and Yonkers Scotch

British beer takes the world by storm. Americans, Australians and troops in India watch for the boats to arrive with the latest consignments while the Empress of all the Russias gives her personal seal of approval to dark stout exported from London.

*Cover of a promotional leaflet produced
by Le Coq to stress the medicinal
properties of Imperial Russian Stout.*

British beer is dismissed as an insular oddity by the rest of the modern world. Yet until tariff barriers and the world-wide swing to lager pulled down the shutters, British beer was exported in great quantities to Europe, Australasia, Asia and the New World of North America. Beer had gone to America with the first settlers and was in great demand until a local industry could be established. British beer imports continued and even grew after the War of Independence. They did not start to fall until the great wave of European immigrants brought with them the skill to brew lager beer, and were extinguished during Prohibition. Early records show that London brewers sent shipments of beer to America and the West Indies in 1695. Samuel Whitbread was exporting beer to New York by 1746, just four years after he had opened his brewery in Chiswell Street. Bristol, with its strong sea links with North America, was also exporting beer by the mid-18th century. British troops sent in an unsuccessful attempt to quell the rebellious colonists ordered 5,000 butts – 108-gallon casks – of strong beer from Felix Calvert and Henry Thrale in London. Trade in beer amounted to some 9,000 barrels a year and most of it was porter, ideally suited to withstand a long sea journey because of its high alcohol and hop levels. George Washington was a keen porter drinker but preferred the home-brewed variety after 1776. Import duties were placed on British beer by some of the new states' governments but sales of British beer grew to 24,000 barrels in 1870 and close to 70,000 by 1910.

The brewers had no control over their exports. There were complaints from the United States that porter was diluted with water and molasses by agents of the British brewers. The Edinburgh firm of William Younger had such excellent sales for its porter and Scotch ale in the US that it had its own agent to look after its affairs. But he could not prevent New York brewers passing off their own products and he was forced to place the following advertisement in the press:

'Having the direct agency for the sale of William Younger and Co's Ales, Edinburgh, Scotland, I would caution the purchasers of Scotch Ale against the many spurious imitations sold, and in many instances bottled, in this city. To escape prosecution for forgery, they have slightly changed the spelling thus – 'Yonkers', retaining the same style of bottles and colour, and otherwise a facsimile of the genuine label.' Yonkers is a district of New York. Younger's India Ale was also popular in New York. The firm's agent expressed his 'acute disappointment' during the hot weather of 1856 that a consignment had not arrived. He ordered 300 casks 'without fail' by October and another 300 by December. When 100 casks of Younger's ale were put on sale in Boston they sold so quickly that the importer told Edinburgh: 'We could have sold readily 500 casks of your ale.' Encouraged by this success, Younger decided to tackle the west coast of the US. An experimental cargo of 60 hogsheads was landed in the city in 1856 by a clipper ship and was sold within hours. The agent there demanded regular monthly shipments and also sold Younger's ale and bottled porter to Sacramento. On one occasion beer was sold straight from the ship *Scotland* when it docked in San Francisco, such was the demand. In 1857 the agent reported: 'The *Hildesheim* arrived some days ago after a fine run of 119 days and discharged a large portion of her cargo in very fine order.' Not all the consignments fared as well. Twenty hogsheads of Younger's ale arrived 'mostly unsound' after a stormy voyage to California in 1857. The following year, in the first attempt to sell ale in Philadelphia, Younger sent a large batch of bottled ale on the aptly named *Tempest* from Liverpool. When the holds were opened after a difficult crossing in rough seas, most of the bottles were found to be broken. The Edinburgh firm had greater success in New Orleans. One batch was sold within minutes of being advertised in the local newspaper:

54

'Expected per ship *Oroondates* from Liverpool, 336 casks Pale Ale, pints and quarts, 172 casks Strong Ale, pints and quarts, Wm Younger and Company, Edinburgh, and for sale by Brulatour & Company, Sole Agents, Old Levee Street.' The Baltimore agent complained to Younger that he had ordered ale but had been sent porter instead, an indication that American tastes were moving away from the dark, heavy beer. Bass India Pale Ale was listed on the menu of the dining cars of the Union Pacific transcontinental railroad and another Burton pale ale, Allsopp's, won prizes in the Centennial Brewers' Exhibition in Philadelphia in 1876.

Tastes in Eastern Europe remained loyal to darker British beers. The Trent Navigation Canal opened up the Baltic trade for the Burton brewers but their ales followed in the wake of London stout and porter. The love of strong, pitch-black London beer was so high that a special type known as 'Imperial' or 'Russian' stout was developed by Barclay Perkins, later to become part of the Courage group. It still produces small amounts of a bottled Imperial Russian Stout with a gravity of 1101 degrees or 10.5 per cent alcohol. Catherine the Great, Empress of all the Russias, was a great devotee of the beer and her patronage helped spread its sales in Russia. It was first brewed at the Anchor Brewery on the Thames embankment in London, the former Thrale's brewery sold to Barclay Perkins. Dr Samuel Johnson had been involved in the sale and commented, with less than his usual verbal elegance, 'We are not here to sell a parcel of boilers and vats, but the potentiality of growing rich beyond the dreams of avarice.' Russian stout certainly made a deal of money for Barclay Perkins but did even better for its bottling company Le Coq, a British-owned firm founded by a Belgian. Le Coq promoted Imperial Russian Stout with great energy and produced pamphlets testifying to its medicinal qualities. A well-publicised gift of 5,000 bottles to Russian hospitals granted Le Coq a warrant to supply the Imperial Court. Herbert Sillem at Le Coq received the following letter from St Petersburg:

A horse-drawn cart in Russia advertising Le Coq's stout.

'Sir, Her Imperial Majesty the Empress Alexandra Prodorovna has been graciously pleased to express to you Her Majesty's kindest thanks for your generous gift of five thousand quarter bottles of stout for hospitals in which the Empress is particularly interested. In conveying to you Her Majesty's gracious thanks I beg to ask you most kindly to forward the stout to Her Majesty's Chancery (Winter Palace, Palace Quay). I beg to excuse my delay in answering your telegram, but that was caused by an indisposition of Her Majesty.' Her Majesty had clearly been neglecting to sup her daily ration of stout. Le Coq's success would have been greater but for the problems of exporting to the Baltic during and after the Napoleonic War, followed by the imposition of tariffs on British goods. The company decided to set up its own brewery at Tartu in Estonia, where it was managed by Oscar Hyde Sillem. The brewery traded successfully until it was burnt down in the First World War and was rebuilt only to

Cold comfort brew: Le Coq's Tartu brewery caught in the snows of winter.

be taken under state control by the Bolshevik government in 1917. After decades of wrangling, compensation of £240,000 was paid by the Soviet government in 1971.

There was even greater demand for Burton-brewed beers once they found their way to Russia and other countries along the Baltic. Baltic beer had to be brewed to a strict timetable. It had to be ready by the end of March of each year as brewing in the late 18th and early 19th centuries was not possible in the summer months. It had to be brewed to a high gravity to survive long and stormy sea voyages and casks had to be battened down not just to stop them pitching around in high seas but also to prevent thirsty sailors from broaching them: there were many complaints from overseas agents concerning half-empty casks. Exporting beer was a highly profitable business if the consignments arrived on time in drinkable condition and were not tampered with. The cost of exporting beer was low. It was treated as ballast by shipping companies and was replaced on the homeward voyages with such essential imports as iron, hemp, tallow and wood. Timber was badly needed by the Burton brewers, along with their competitors in other areas. Casks were not returned from the overseas markets (they were pilfered by other brewers) and quality wood, Russian oak in particular, was essential to the coopering trade. A large ancillary coopering business flourished in Burton and survived until the advent of the metal cask in the middle of the 20th century.

The disruption of the Baltic trade sent British brewers in search of new markets. Hodgson of London, as we have seen, was the first to exploit the India market with a new pale ale. Burton's hard water supply was ideally suited to pale ale production and soon clippers were ploughing through the waves with their holds packed with casks and bottles of 'India Pale Ale'. The term survives to this day. Although trade with India has long since ceased, several brewers produce IPA for the home market. Few of them match the strength of the original with the possible exception of the bottled Worthington White Shield, marketed by Bass as 'the original India Pale Ale'. Trade with India, with its insatiable thirst for quenching beers in the torrid heat, grew rapidly and attracted brewers from other parts of Britain. By 1833 Allsopp and Bass beers from Burton were joined on the docks by Barclay and Charrington from London and Tennent from Glasgow. In 1840 some 20,000 barrels of ale were exported to India and the business rose to a peak of 217,000 barrels in 1870. By 1860 production of pale ale was the 'first consideration' at Allsopp's brewery and its impact was being felt at home as well as abroad. Simonds of Reading began to brew 'a novel kind of beer, pale ale, for export' in 1834. Simonds used its contacts with the British Army based at Aldershot to export beer to India, Malta, Gibraltar, Egypt, Cyprus and South Africa. Younger of Edinburgh had supplied bottled beer in 1855 to British troops fighting at Alma, Inkermann and Balaclava during the Crimean War. The strength of export beers at the time can be seen in a complaint to Younger from an agent in Calcutta in

1858: 'Your beer is well known for its body. This is an obstacle to its becoming a favourite brand; it takes so long to ripen. The few casks of your last lot were fully 18 months before sufficiently ripe to drink.' In spite of that small setback, British beer exports in that year were worth £2,000,000.

Trade to India declined after 1870 as local breweries began to meet the demand. But new markets were opening up in Australia and New Zealand. The gold rush in Australia in the 1850s sent 400,000 British emigrants in search of wealth. They needed refreshment in that harsh, hot climate and the British brewers hurried to their aid, if a minimum 68-day voyage by the fastest clipper could be described as hurrying. From Australia it was a shorter journey to New Zealand. British beers were acclaimed there. In July 1857 Younger received an urgent appeal from its New Zealand agent: 'We want show cards. Quality of ale approved of. Keep us supplied and we will do good business. We have the only underground cellar in Wellington which is excellently adapted for malt liquors. Nelson Goldfields going ahead and only requires a spring to induce thousands to try their luck at them.' In August 1858 the same agent wrote: 'Your ale much liked and well-suited to our climate', a note that has a somewhat plaintive tone when you consider the rapid adoption of lager in the Antipodes in the 20th century.

Lager arrived in Australia in 1885 when two Germans founded the Gambrinus brewery in Melbourne. They were soon followed by the American Foster brothers who started a second lager brewery in the city. Castlemaine started to brew in Brisbane in 1889. In 1900 a Swiss brewer named Conrad Breutsch was brought to New Zealand specifically to produce lager. Ironically, he brewed at the Captain Cook Brewery in Auckland, named in honour of the Yorkshire sea captain who had first brewed a rough ale in New Zealand to cure his crew of scurvy. Lager was now entering its ascendancy in Australasia and North America, and the First World War and attacks from German submarines on the British merchant fleet finally killed off exports of British beer.

British beer did go to sea again in the Second World War. When the Prime Minister, Sir Winston Churchill, heard that British troops in the Far East were rationed to a mere three bottles of beer a month he demanded that action be taken to increase the supply. George Brown, head brewer at Truman in London, was serving with the London Scottish Regiment in Italy. He was transferred to the Royal Navy Volunteer Reserve (Special Branch), promoted to Lieutenant Commander and sent to Canada to set up a brewing unit on board the Royal Navy amenity ship *Menestheus*. The floating brewery had two brewers, two petty officers, eight ratings and five Chinese stewards. Beer was brewed from distilled sea water, malt extract, hop concentrate and yeast, rather like a modern home-brew kit. The beer was known, with gallow's humour, as Davy Jones Ale and sold at ninepence (4p) a pint. It was sold to troops in the Pacific and Indian Ocean and NAAFIs displayed a special poster announcing:

Something from the OLD COUNTRY!
A Breath from BRITAIN!!. . .
ENGLISH MILD ALE
brewed in
Davy Jones Brewery – 'The World's Only Floating Brewery!'

Once again, British beer was refreshing the troops overseas.

CHAPTER SIX

Heavy Going

Scotland carves out its own distinctive beer style to the approval of Robert Burns. The large commercial brewers of the Lowlands come to dominate the market and the Scots develop an early taste for European-style lager.

A handsome tall font for serving traditional Scottish beer.

Scotland has carved out its own distinctive contribution to British beer. Beer north of the border looks and tastes different. It has different names for mild and bitter – the Scots call them 'light' and 'heavy' – and they are served by an air pressure system that is hardly seen in England. The beers are brewed in a different way and traditional beers have been under attack from lager for a much longer period than the rest of the British Isles. The reasons for the differences are not based on Celtic cussedness but are the result of the distorted and often tragic course of Scotland's history. For centuries, brewing in Scotland followed a similar path to England and Wales. Beer was a monastic and domestic necessity but barley was not always easy to grow in some of the harsher and more isolated northern areas. When it could be cultivated it was of a variety called 'bigg' that was not best suited for malting. As a result Scottish beer often had a poor reputation. Thomas Kirke from England reported on a trip to Scotland in the early 18th century: 'Their drink is ale, made of beer malt, and tunned up in a small vessel, called a cogue; after it has stood a few hours, they drink it out of the cogue, yest and all; the better sort brew it in large quantities, and drink it in wooden queighs, but it is sorry stuff.'

As a result of the 'Auld Alliance' with France, the gentry quaffed wine. Gin made some inroads but in Scotland, of course, there was another spirit popular with the masses. In the late 18th century records show that whisky was drunk in large quantities. A labourer would put away a small bottle of neat whisky at a sitting. Whisky was cheap and its popularity meant that its manufacturers could demand the best of the barley. As the Industrial Revolution made its impact in Scotland, commercial breweries developed in all the major towns of the country, but they tended to congregate in the Lowlands where the best barley was grown. And so did the great majority of the working population, swelled by the hapless victims of the Highland clearances. From the Highlands came the taste for *uisge beatha*, the water of life, a spirit that owed its origins to beer, for whisky is a distillation of unhopped beer. The love for whisky and its cheapness meant that brewers had to wait in the queue for good malt behind the distillers. Gradually the brewing industry concentrated in the Lowlands in order to get its share of the barley. Alloa, Edinburgh and Glasgow became the major brewing centres. It was this geographic oddity, a vast country served by breweries based predominantly in the far south, with all the costs of transport and the problems of keeping beer in good condition, that helped fuel the drive towards mergers and centralised production. Scotland today gets the great bulk of its beer from just two giants, Scottish and Newcastle (better known as Younger and McEwan), and Tennent Caledonian. And Tennent in turn is owned by the Bass group.

As commercial brewing took root in the 18th century, the quality of beer started to improve, though the ramshackle nature of some brewhouses were clearly hazardous, as one sad tale in the Edinburgh press shows: 'One Margaret Strachan, who was to have been married this week, was brewing Ale for the Marriage, but unfortunately fell backwards into a Tub of boiling wort, whereby she was miserably scalded to death.' Robert Tennent, a publican, and William Younger, a farmer's son, had better fortune with their first small concerns in Glasgow and Leith even though these early commercial businesses were dismissed derisorily as 'kitchen breweries'. William Younger's kitchen firm prospered because his beer was good and because he was able to invest in the best equipment and materials due to his other activity. Younger was an excise officer, vigilantly seeking and detaining smugglers of brandy, tea and coffee and he was well rewarded by the harassed authorities. The major impact on the beer scene was made, however, by his son Archibald Campbell, who set up his own brewery in Edinburgh.

His ambition was to produce a distinctive Scottish beer that would stand comparison with the best from England. The main beer of the time was known as 'twopenny', a cheap, thin beverage of poor repute. The *Edinburgh Evening Courant* did not think much of the product or the dubious 'assistance' given to it by some publicans:

'Soft Ale is an homogeneous Liquor, which affords a pleasant Undulation of the Spirits, with some sensation of Weight and Flatulency upon the Stomach . . . Let me exhort my country-men to brew their Ale from the softest Water, the palest Malt, and the most fragrant Hops, always free from that forced, unnatural strength which the Publican finds so advantageous in Trade; and I am persuaded this Drinkable would soon be thought worthy the Notice of the best Families in England.'

Archibald Campbell Younger brewed an ale that challenged the claret swigged in Edinburgh taverns and the whisky, much of it illicit, being downed in seedy dram shops. Younger's ale became the smart drink of the city in such celebrated drinking places as Johnnie Dowie's Tavern. Chambers' *Traditions of Edinburgh*, published in 1825, reported:

'Johnnie Dowie's was chiefly celebrated for ale – Younger's Edinburgh ale – a potent fluid which almost glued the lips of the drinker together, and of which few, therefore, could despatch more than a bottle. John, a sleek, quiet-looking man in a last-century style of attire, always brought in the liquor himself, decanted it carefully, drank a glass to the health of the company and then retired.' Writers, artists, even the great economist Adam Smith, congregated in Johnnie Dowie's. A poet called Hunter of Blackness was so fired with enthusiasm by the local brew that he penned the lines:

> O, Dowie's ale! thou art the thing
> That gars us crack, and gars us sing,
> Cast by our cares, our wants a' fling
>   Frae us wi' anger;
> Thou e'en mak'st passion tak' the wing.
>   Or thou wilt bang 'er.

The poem was wrongly attributed to Robert Burns. But the great poet was a regular customer and when Johnnie Dowie died his place was renamed Burns Tavern.

The Youngers, Tennent and the other prospering commercial brewers of the Lowlands were developing a distinctive beer style. They imported the finest English malts to supplement the local variety. Hops were not grown in Scotland and the cost of bringing them from Kent and the other English hop-growing counties meant that they were used more sparingly. The brewers were alive to developments in the south, though. They not only sold Scottish ales in London but added porter to their portfolios. The Anderston Brewery Company of Glasgow was the first Scottish brewer to attempt to reproduce the dark beer of the English capital. It hired Nathaniel Chivers who had brewed in London and for Guinness in Dublin. The terms of the contract could have been drawn up by the secret service, as Chivers letter of agreement of September 1775 shows:

'Gentlemen, Having engaged to impart to you the London method of brewing strong beer, commonly called porter, and in order to give evidence of my knowledge therein, have further engaged to brew such beer at your brewery as shall have the London flavour and keeping qualities, for which purpose you have engaged to pay me £25 sterling as my expenses to and from Glasgow, upon condition that I do not impart the art of brewing to any other in your place and neighbourhood, which I have approved; and do hereby covenant and promise, that I will not communicate that art to any but you and your brewing servant, under the penalty of one hundred guineas – N. Chivers.'

Chivers was a double agent. He was paid a total of £300 by the Anderston company but he also taught a Glasgow competitor, John Struthers of Gallowgate, the art of porter brewing. Robert Meiklejohn of Alloa also employed a London brewer while the two Younger companies, as a prelude to eventual merger, announced in a press advertisement in November 1806:

'TO PORTER DEALERS. Archibald Campbell Younger and William Younger have commenced Brewers of Porter under the firm of A.C. and W. Younger. To enable them to obtain a complete knowledge of the art of making the article, they have engaged a London brewer of great professional ability, and they are happy to say that he has succeeded in producing porter that will vie in every respect with the best that can be imported from London.'

The 19th century was a time of expansion and consolidation for the commercial city brewers. They bought up most of the surviving small country breweries. The railway meant that they could sell their products to most of Scotland and England and they opened offices and warehouses in London and the other English cities. Tyneside in particular became a happy hunting ground for Scottish beer; when a Geordie calls for a 'Scotch' he expects to be served with beer not whisky. The brewers of Glasgow, Edinburgh and Alloa were well placed to export their beers overseas. Younger's adventures and misadventures in the export trade were noted in the previous chapter. The company was not alone. Tennent in Glasgow on the west coast was one of the first British brewers to supply North America. McEwan of Edinburgh did not start brewing until 1856 but rapidly built up a substantial trade with Australia and New Zealand in the 1860s. When Burton and London began to supply India with pale ale, the Scottish companies hurried to join them but their fame, and their fortunes, were made not so much by copies of English bitter and porter but by the rare, dry, lightly hopped palate of Scotch or export ale. But Scotch ale faced competition from a new style of beer in the 1890s called lager. Tennent of Glasgow started to brew lager at Wellpark in 1888. The company was helped by Pasteur's studies of fermentation and the distinction between 'top fermenting' yeast for British beer and 'bottom fermenting' yeast for the new beers of Pilsen, Bavaria and Dortmund, and further aided by the introduction of refrigeration. A custom-built lager brewery was opened in Glasgow in 1906. John Jeffrey of Edinburgh was another early lager pioneer. Just why the Scots became so addicted to lager at such an early stage, a good 50 years ahead of the English, has never been satisfactorily explained. Pilsener style beers from Europe were exported to Scotland from the 1870s and sales grew by five times between 1880 and 1895. They could just as easily have been exported south of the border, but the English showed no interest in continental beer. Alfred Chapman suggested in the *Brewers' Guardian* in 1896 that the success of lager was due to the fact that the Scots had started to travel to Europe and the United States and had picked up a taste for lager. Not all Scots travelled purely for pleasure. One of the country's main exports has always been people in search of work. Those who did eventually return from Europe, North America and even Australasia would have brought with them a taste for bottom-fermented beer. Scotsmen who stayed at home had a habit of drinking beer as a 'chaser' with whisky. Perhaps the lighter palate of lager did not over-power the delicate flavour of good whisky. The answer could also lie with the fact that the distinction between the pale Scottish ales of the late 19th century and lager was more blurred than between English beers and the European style. Scottish beers were fermented traditionally at much lower temperatures than in England. While warm fermentation lasts for five or six days, in Scotland it could last for up to three weeks. The lower temperature meant that the yeast did not create the great frothy head so evident in a typical English brewery. With lower hop rates, the end result was a beer that was something of a hybrid, not by definition lager but closer to it than the new breed of English 'running' or draught beers with their sharp hoppy edge.

The arrival of lager did not mean the end of Scotch ales. They survive and the current demand for such splendid beers as Belhaven's, Maclay's, McEwan's 80 shilling, Lorimer's and Broughton's is increasing. But lager served further to distort the already concentrated nature of Scottish brewing. The heavy capital outlay needed to brew lager favoured the bigger companies. Mergers and closures marked the development of the Scottish industry throughout the present century and proliferated in the 1960s and 70s. Such famous brewing names as Aitchison, Aitken, Bernard, Blair, Jeffrey and George and

Robert Younger disappeared. Tennent of Glasgow had bought several west of Scotland breweries and paid the price for getting bigger by being merged with Caledonian Breweries to become Tennent Caledonian, part of the Bass group. Younger and McEwan had merged in the 1930s to become Scottish Breweries and in 1960 cemented its long-standing links with the north-east of England by merging with Newcastle Breweries, the biggest amalgamation in Scottish brewing history. Allied Breweries, Britain's second largest beer group, owned the Alloa Brewery and Watney, part of the vast Grand Metropolitan group, bought the Drybrough Brewery near Edinburgh in 1965 and then sold its brewing interests in Scotland to Allied in 1987. The most controversial of all the takeovers came when Whitbread bought Campbell, Hope and King of Edinburgh in 1968. The company brewed some of the most admired and popular beers in Scotland. It was also heavily involved in whisky blending, which may have been the main attraction for Whitbread. The English company closed the brewery and supplied English beers to the Scottish market, a piece of gross insensitivity that still rankles. To this day many Scots living in England refuse to drink in Whitbread pubs.

Scottish brewing has followed a different path to England and Wales in another way. There is little 'tied trade', with pubs or bars directly owned by the breweries. Since the late 19th century Scottish brewers preferred a loan arrangement with bars rather than direct ownership. Loans on favourable terms are given to owners and managers in return for a commitment to take the bulk of their supplies – beer, lager, wines and spirits – from the lending brewer. It does not mean there is any greater choice, given the financial power and the market dominance of Scottish & Newcastle and Tennent Caledonian. Drinkers have to search hard for beers from other companies.

Visitors to Scotland will have to have a crash course in brewing linguistics. Not only are mild and bitter called 'light' and 'heavy' but they also appear under other titles. Light is also called 60 shilling, heavy is 70 shilling and strong ale is 80 shilling. This system harks back to the 1870s when beer was

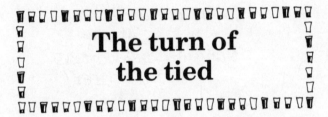

CHAPTER SEVEN

The turn of the tied

Beer acts, tax and the temperance movement force radical change on the brewing industry. Publican-brewers go into sharp decline and the commercial companies buy up pubs in order to ensure a steady trade for their products.

Edward Greene, the Suffolk brewer who ran Greene King, died in 1891 and was paid the following tribute by the London evening paper *The Star*: 'He was one of the first country brewers to discover that beer need not be vile, black turgid stuff, but brewed a bright amber-coloured liquid of Burton type, which he sold at a shilling per gallon and made a fortune'. Greene had made his fortune not only by brewing splendid beer but by selling it in his own pubs. By the year of his death Greene King owned 250 tied houses. The beer may have been of the 'Burton type' but the tenants of the pubs were not allowed to sell genuine Burton beer. The tenants were truly tied, hand and foot, to the brewery and were allowed only to sell its products. The tied house system was not confined to country brewers. The major commercial companies in London and other great conurbations had set the trend. The success of Burton ale had frightened the pants off the rest of the nation's brewers.

The public wanted the new pale, hoppy beers produced by Bass and Worthington. The Burton brewers were happy to oblige. Bass by 1900 was one of the wonders of the Victorian world, the archetypal entrepreneur. The company produced 1,500,000 barrels of beer that year on its 145 acre site, with a workforce of 3,500. With a small army of gentlemen 'representatives' on the road to cajole publicans and the railways to speed supplies, Bass was able to meet an insatiable demand. The London and Home Counties brewers faced disaster unless they could meet the Burton challenge and switch from porter to pale ale. Some, as we have seen, opened second breweries in Burton but the real need was to convert their home bases to pale ale. Pasteur had come to their aid with his *Etudes sur la Bière* and soon translations were required reading in every brewery. When

Horace Brown FRS finished his studies at the Royal College of Chemistry in the 1860s and returned to his job at Worthington's Burton brewery, he found a disturbing reluctance to use his new found knowledge 'due to the fear that the display of any chemical apparatus might suggest to customers the horrible suspicion that the beer was being "doctored".' But within a few years every brewery had a microscope once the managements had read and imbibed Pasteur and knew that they had to prevent infections. In 1895 the *Journal of the Institute of Brewing* told the Yorkshire Institute that the time had gone when the brewery could be regarded as 'the last resource for a young man when, having failed for the Army, the Church, or one of the learned professions, his premium is paid and he is shipped off to some pupil-taking brewery with the idea that "at least we can make a brewer of him".' The journal stressed that the modern brewer should be 'essentially a chemist, as brewing is practically the conversion of certain substances into certain chemically different substances by what is more or less a chemical process.' The day of the brewery laboratory had arrived. And it was there not just to prevent infections and maintain a pure strain of yeast but to treat the water with chemicals to make them hard like Burton liquor.

The southern brewers could now brew Burton-style beer – bitter as it came to be called. But they had to get the original Burton beers out of southern pubs. Changes to the 1830 Beer Act had ruined many publican brewers and their houses had been bought for a song by the bigger firms. Now the race was on to buy as many 'public houses', a Victorian expression, as possible. Large sums of money were required and the major brewers followed the path set by Guinness in 1886 and became public companies with shareholders. Two hundred breweries 'went public' by 1890. The result was that the price of pubs in the south shot up as the brewers scrambled over one another to grab as much real estate as they could. Smaller brewers were priced out of the market and disappeared or were taken over. Even the big brewers faced difficulties. Before the stampede to buy property they had adopted the Scottish system of the 'loan tie'. In 1896 when Barclay Perkins became a public company it was owed £2 million by publicans. The figure had increased to £3 million by 1900. When the property bubble burst in London thousands of publicans became insolvent and could not repay their loans. Barclay Perkins' shares fell by 40 per cent and the company had to be restructured. Ind Coope and Allsopp were in even direr straits and were put into the hands of the receiver. Whitbread, Charrington and Watney all felt the draught; Watney merged with Combe Reid in 1898. In 1904 Cosmo Bonsor, the chairman of Watney Combe Reid, explained the problems of recent years: 'This company carried on practically two businesses. They were manufacturers and sellers of beer. This part of the business was as good as ever. It was the other portion of the business in which they dealt in the securities of licensed houses, that the losses came from.' The brewers hurried to end the loan-tie arrangement. The direct ownership of pubs, with assured sales for their products, was the order of the day. By 1900, 90 per cent of pubs were brewery owned. The brewers needed them as a hedge against other problems. A recession in the 1890s and rising unemployment had created a slump in beer sales. The situation was not made easier by the plausible propaganda of a powerful late-Victorian temperance movement and the tacit support of the Liberal Party, which was imbued with strong anti-alcohol and anti-brewer prejudices. The misery and squalor of life in the new urban areas created by the manufacturing revolution had created a climate for over-indulgence in alcohol to drown the sorrows of the impoverished working class. The temperance movement, through meetings, pamphlets and songs, called for heavier taxes on beer, tougher licensing laws and urged drinkers to 'sign the pledge'. Its influence spread even to the armed forces. A Regimental Temperance Association was formed and gave 'campaign medals' to soldiers who signed the pledge. The association newspaper *Our Chronicle* mixed details of temperant events – 'tea and refreshing lime juice were served by the Colonel's lady' – with grim warnings in even grimmer verse to those still unwise enough to imbibe:

> Dare to say 'No' when you're tempted to drink,
> Pause for a moment, my brave boy, and think –
> Think of the wrecks upon life's ocean tossed
> For answering 'Yes' without counting the cost.
> Think of the mother who bore you in pain!
> Think of the tears that will fall like the rain;
> Think of the heart & how cruel the blow;
> Think of her love & at once answer 'No!'
> Think of lone graves both unswept and unknown, –
> Hiding fond hopes that were fair as your own;
> Think of proud forms now for ever laid low,
> That still might be here had they learnt to say 'No!'
> Think of the demon that lurks in the bowl,
> Driving to ruin both body & soul;
> Think of all this as life's journey you go,
> And when you're assailed by the tempter
> SAY 'NO!'

A Liberal bill in 1908, with the vociferous support of the temperance movement, threatened to cut back the number of public houses by 30,000. The brewing journals complained that the government was 'hounding the trade out of existence'. In the event, the measure was thrown out by the House of Lords. The bill also attempted to ban barmaids. This was another sop to the temperance kill-joys who thought that brave lads would not be so keen to enter dens of iniquity if there were no female tempt-resses behind the bars. Thousands of barmaids demonstrated in Hyde Park against their planned demise and the plan was dropped.

Beer duty was increased in 1900 to help pay for the Boer War. The brewers, staunch defenders of Queen and Country, grumbled about this extra burden. Beer duty had been introduced by Gladstone in his 1880 budget. Until then duty had been paid on malt but the budget switched tax to beer. The decision was momentous for another reason. As Gladstone pointed out, his measure would 'give the brewer the right to

76

brew from whatever he pleases, and he will have a perfect choice both of his materials and his methods. I am of the opinion that it is of enormous advantage to the community to liberate an industry so large as this with regard to the choice of those materials. Our intention is to admit all materials whatever to perfectly free and open competition.' The result was a decline in the malt content of beer and the use of inferior materials. It would be absurd to suggest that beer prior to 1880 had been simon pure and all-malt. For centuries drinkers had complained about adulteration. The use of molasses was widespread. But Gladstone now enshrined in law the right of brewers to adulterate their beers, whereas in Germany and parts of Scandinavia brewers to this day are allowed to use only malt, though the German Pure Beer Law, the *Reinheitsgebot*, has been ruled a 'restraint of trade' by the European Court.

The effect of Gladstone's change was neatly summed up by Dr Shidrovitch, a leading brewery chemist, in the 1911 edition of the *Encyclopaedia Britannica*: 'Substitutes enable the brewer appreciably to increase his turnover: he can now make more beer in a given time from the same plant. The brewer has found that brewery operations are simplified and accelerated by the use of a certain proportion of substitutes. Certain classes of substitutes too are somewhat cheaper than malt, and in view of the keenness of modern competition, it is not to be wondered at that the brewer should resort to every legitimate means at his disposal to keep down costs . . . The light beers in vogue today are less alcoholic, more lightly hopped and more quickly brewed than beers of the last generation, and in this respect are somewhat less stable and more liable to deteriorate than the latter were.' While the good doctor was careful not to split his infinitives he was reticent about the 'certain classes of substitutes' brewers were able to use. Sugar was the main new and cheap ingredient. In Scotland for example brewers were using 80,000 bushel equivalents of sugar by 1886 or 4 per cent of total materials. Ten years later the figure had risen to nearly 230,000 bushel equivalents of sugar. Some brewers were using up to 10 per cent sugar, especially in cheaper beers. Other materials, known as adjuncts, were also gleefully seized on by the brewers. Rice, wheat, corn starch and unmalted barley began to change the palate of the nation's beer and to boost the profits of the brewers. The image of the brewer in the 20th century has not always been high, as a famous song from the 1930s depression years made clear:

> Oh, I'm the man, the very fat man
> That waters the workers' beer.
> Yes, I'm the man, the very fat man
> That waters the workers' beer.
> And what care I if it makes 'em ill,
> If it makes 'em 'orribly queer.
> I've a car, a yacht and an aeroplane
> 'Cos I waters the workers' beer.

The turn of the century had seen a number of innovations, not all of them beneficial to the taste and quality of beer. Small amounts of beer had been put into bottles since the 18th century but bottled beer production soared with the invention of machine-blown bottles secured with first a stopper and later a sealed metal cap. As with beer in casks, bottled beer matured naturally in its container and threw a slight yeasty sediment. Pasteur made change possible. His studies were a mixed blessing for beer drinkers. He had shown the way to root out infections and brew cleaner and purer beer. But he also introduced the method of heating beer, milk and other beverages to make them completely sterile. 'Pasteurisation' may be necessary in a cow shed but its use in breweries produced beers with a tell-tale burnt sugar taste that masked the true smack of malt and hops. Bottled beer became a filtered and pasteurised drink that was given a fake sparkle with a burst of 'carbonic gas', better known today as carbon dioxide. The new style beer pleased the brewers as a result of its sterility and longer shelf life, a fact that was not lost on them later in the century. Breweries were changing, too. The Victorian 'tower' brewery was now the vogue, with production flowing logically from floor to floor, starting with the mashing of the wort at the top to conditioning and cask filling at the

A traditional tower brewery, with the brewing process flowing from floor to floor.

bottom. Handsome examples of the tower brewery can be seen at Harvey's of Lewes in Sussex and Hook Norton in Oxfordshire. Wooden vessels were giving way to metal. The union room system of fermentation was becoming confined to Burton as most brewers preferred to use just one vessel for the vital stage when the hopped wort was transformed into alcohol. The yeast was skimmed from the top of the fermenters, pressed and stored for future use. The southern brewers in particular favoured this system in order to produce 'running' bitters as quickly as possible in order to ward off the competitive threat from Burton. In Yorkshire a different system had developed. The stone square system was so called because the fermenting vessels were originally made of local stone. The square is made up of two chambers. The lower section is filled with wort and when fermentation starts the yeast rises into the top chamber through a manhole. The wort is then pumped into the top chamber and vigorously mixed with the yeast. When fermentation is finished, the beer runs back into the bottom chamber. The natural carbon dioxide produced during fermentation is trapped in the square. It is claimed by Yorkshire drinkers, with their religious devotion to the way beer is served, that the high concentration of gas produces a pint with the thick head or collar that is rooted in northern drinking.

Whether beer was brewed by the Burton union, Yorkshire square or skimming methods, British drinkers were devoted to draught beers that underwent a natural second fermentation in the cask, which developed a distinctive rich, hoppy palate. The post-Pasteur revolution stopped short of moving to lager-style production, with slower, cooler fermentation and lighter rates of hopping. There were attempts to brew lager when the Prince of Wales made much-publicised trips to German spa towns and newspapers were filled with stories of all things German, including their beers. Allsopp began to brew lager at Burton in 1899 and its near neighbour and future partner, Ind Coope, experimented with a lager beer called Burgomaster. (The brewers' determination to give English lager fake German names was not confined to the 1970s.) There was little demand for lager though, except in Wales where the Wrexham Lager Company found a slot in a market where dark mild ale was the predominant drink. The Wrexham company, emulating the origins of bottom fermented lager beer, had decided to store its product in ice-filled caves until it was persuaded that refrigeration was an easier method.

Prosperity returned to the industry in 1912 when beer sales increased but new problems arrived with the outbreak of the First World War. The restrictions on the sale of alcohol under the Defence of the Realm Act (which are detailed in the chapter *Haven't you got homes to go to?*) were allied to a lowering of beer strength in order to control and safeguard raw materials. By the end of the war the average gravity of beer had sunk to just 1031 degrees, about 3 per cent alcohol, some 20 degrees less than at the turn of the century. Not surprisingly beer consumption slumped during the war from 35 million barrels in 1914 to 19 million by the end as drinkers showed their distaste for the 'near beer' served up as a result of government legislation. The strength of beer increased after the war but it would never return to its Victorian and Edwardian levels. In 1924 a new method of raising duty was brought in. Instead of a standard rate on all beers, duty was levied according to the gravity of a brew: the higher the gravity, the greater the level of duty, a further encouragement to brew weaker beer.

Beer was struggling. The war-time restrictions, followed by rising and endemic unemployment in the 1920s and 30s, killed off many smaller brewers. There were 3,000 brewing companies in 1920. The number had fallen to just 1,000 by the outbreak of World War Two. The industry dug deep into its pocket to attract badly needed drinkers. Pubs were modernised in an effort to bring in a 'better class' of customer. Advertising, from the mundane 'Beer is Best' to the brilliant Guinness campaigns – which made the slogan 'My goodness my Guinness' part of the English language and the toucan a national character – did its best to create demand. War was once again to disrupt and distort the industry but even before the outbreak of hostilities a small event in Surrey acted as the harbinger of a massive post-war upheaval. In 1936 the East Sheen Tennis Club had complained to Watney that its draught beer did not keep well as little of it was drunk during the week and it had become sour by the week-end when it was in demand. Watney had been experimenting with a new kind of beer for overseas sale. Instead of running live beer into casks to mature, the beer was filtered and pasteurised, placed in a sealed container called a keg and pumped with carbon dioxide to prolong its life. Watney supplied it to the tennis club. The beer was called Red Barrel.

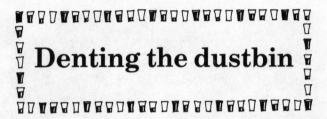

CHAPTER EIGHT

Denting the dustbin

Takeovers and mergers in the 1960s and 1970s reduce drinkers' choice and lead to the switch to mass-produced and heavily promoted keg beers. Drinkers fight back and demand traditional beer through the Campaign for Real Ale.

Happy topers at a CAMRA beer festival.

The Second World War had an even greater impact on the brewing industry than the First. Gravities of beer were again reduced substantially by the government to save raw materials and inferior unmalted 'adjuncts' were let loose in the mash tun. Brewers' sales were restricted to small regions. Thousands of pubs were destroyed by bombs and an unknown number of publicans lost their lives either at home or in the armed forces. In spite of the problems of aerial bombardment and the blackout, the government encouraged beer production and the profits of the brewers increased as a result. They were men who did well out of the war.

The war stamped an indelible mark on the industry and its post-war development. The poor quality of beer during the war was compounded in the 1950s by an influx of new and inexperienced publicans with little or no knowledge of keeping and serving draught beer. As a result there was a substantial consumer switch to bottled beer, most of it pasteurised and artificially carbonated but reliable. Such brands as Guinness and Double Diamond were heavily promoted. The swing to bottled beer was a boon for the bigger brewers who had the funds to invest in new, sophisticated bottling lines and to advertise their products. Smaller companies were in the doldrums. The situation was ripe for the orgy of takeovers and mergers of the 1960s and 70s that gave the industry its biggest shake-up since the arrival of the hop.

The large regional brewers drew the wrong conclusions from declining sales of draught beer. Instead of training publicans in its safe keeping and promoting it as energetically as bottled beer, they began to experiment with a new type of bulk packaged beer known as keg. Watney's Red Barrel had been the first of the

THE MAN WHO ASKED FOR
A PINT OF RED BARREL

breed and now Bass, Courage, Ind Coope, Whitbread and the other major companies started to brew rival products. Keg is bottled beer in a bigger container. When the beer has been fermented, it is chilled, filtered, pasteurised and heavily carbonated and run into metal kegs – 'sealed dustbins' as one disgruntled critic called them. In the pub the beer is pumped to the bar by gas pressure. The result is a product with a 'long shelf life' as the marketing departments say. In other words, unlike traditional draught beer, it stays in a drinkable condition for several months, rather than just a few days. It is cold, fizzy and has the 'burnt sugar' taste created by pasteurisation. It lacks the rounded, mature taste of a beer that naturally conditions in the cask. But it is enormously profitable.

In order to gain the maximum advantage from keg beer, which was advertised with great elan in order to stimulate consumer 'demand', the regional brewers had to transform themselves into national combines. 'Rationalisation' and 'economies of scale' were the phrases on the lips of the new breed of brewing moguls who were concerned less with quality and tradition and more with maximising profits. They were encouraged by the publication of Professor John Vaizey's weighty tome *The Brewing Industry 1886–1951*. He argued that the only viable future for brewing lay in large centres of production alongside the emerging motorway network. Significantly, Vaizey's book appeared in 1960, the year when a Canadian entrepreneur named Eddie Taylor launched a frantic, whirlwind raid on British brewing, as if hell-bent on proving the efficacy of the good professor's theory. Taylor was owner of Carling Black Label lager and he wanted Britain to drink it. To achieve that aim he needed breweries and pubs. In just ten months he bought 12 breweries in Scotland and the north of England and created a regional giant called Northern United Breweries. Most of the breweries were closed and their beers disappeared. The tragic trend had been set. In 1961, Taylor cajoled the mighty London firm, Charrington, into joining the group and two years later he bought Tennents in Glasgow. In 1967 he set the seal on his coup. Bass, which included Worthington and Mitchells & Butlers, joined the new conglomerate. Bass Charrington, the first national brewing giant, owned 10,000 pubs, had breweries strategically placed throughout England, Scotland and Wales and enjoyed an annual turnover of £900 million. Eddie Taylor controlled 20 per cent of the brewing industry. Carling had found its outlets.

The other regional brewers were terrified of being swamped by Bass. They hurried to go national too. In 1961 Ind Coope, Ansells and Tetley merged to form Allied Breweries with 7,600 pubs. Whitbread closed 15 breweries between 1960 and 1971 as it turned itself into a national giant. Even Samuel Whitbread's pride, joy and epoch-making brewery in London's Chiswell Street ceased to brew. Southern distribution was concentrated at a vast new keg-only plant built alongside the M1 motorway at Luton. Watney Mann had been created in 1958 by the merging of two famous London brewing companies, Watney Combe Reid, and Mann, Crossman and Paulin. The new group snapped up breweries in the North, the Midlands and East Anglia and also bought the substantial spirits group International Distillers and Vintners. In 1971 it failed to buy another London-based brewing group, Truman, Hanbury and Buxton, which fell to Maxwell Joseph's Grand Metropolitan leisure group for £49 million. The following year, Grand Met bought Watney for £413 million. It was the biggest takeover in British history and created a brewing division called Watney Mann and Truman.

Courage, yet another legendary London brewer, merged with Barclay Perkins in 1955 and then with Simonds of Reading in 1960. It was still too southern-based to be counted as a national combine and was vulnerable to takeover itself. In 1970 it achieved national status when it bought John Smiths of Tadcaster in Yorkshire. As with Watney, Courage paid the price: two years later it was bought and became the brewing division of the cigarettes, crisps and HP sauce group, Imperial Tobacco. In the North, Scottish Brewers and Newcastle Breweries merged in 1960 and formed Scottish and Newcastle. Although the group owned only a small fraction of the tied houses of its rivals, it established itself as a national combine through its vigorous exploitation of the free trade, where its keg beer Tartan became a brand leader.

Britain was now dominated by the 'Big Six' brewing groups. They owned half the country's tied houses and they held sway increasingly in the free trade, including clubs, through a policy of offering landlords and club managers substantial low-interest loans to improve their premises in return for an agreement to take their supplies of beer, wines and spirits only from the brewery lending the money. Keg beer production soared. In 1959, on the eve of the great takeover scramble, keg accounted for just 1 per cent of beer production. By 1976, 63 per cent of beer was in keg – and 20 per cent of it was in the form of lager. Traditional draught beer was now a sideline save for the handful of small local and regional breweries that had survived the holocaust and continued doggedly to brew the type of beer they and their customers preferred.

The great savings for the national combines foreseen by Professor Vaizey had not materialised. Sharply rising costs of fuel negated the benefits of centralised beer production. Shifting bulk beer around the motorway system became an expensive business. The big brewers passed on the costs to the hapless consumers. In many parts of the country they had little option but to drink in Big Six pubs. National brands cost substantially more than local ones. And local brands were often hard to find. At the end of the merger and takeover scramble, the number of beer brands had been halved.

And then the consumer struck back. When four drinkers in the Manchester area formed the Campaign for Real Ale in 1972 they did not expect to spawn a national pub revolt that would shake the brewing industry to its foundations. But by the late seventies CAMRA had more than 20,000 members and was described by (Lord) Michael Young, chairman of the National Consumer Council in 1976, as 'the most successful consumer movement in Europe'. It was a case of David stunning if not slaying Goliath. The Big Six brewers were immensely rich and

Monty Python actor and writer Terry Jones recalled the days of the 'ale conner' when he tested the quality of the beer at a CAMRA festival.

powerful and yet they found themselves ridiculed by a pip-squeak organisation always desperately short of funds and with just a handful of full-time officials. The brewers thought at first that CAMRA would quickly run out of steam. They reckoned without the anger and determination of its grass-roots members, organised nationally into branches and regions, who spent their spare time lobbying brewers, organising marches and protests, writing letters to newspapers and MPs and producing lists of outlets that still sold traditional ale for the annual *Good Beer Guide*. CAMRA punctured the pretensions of the big brewers and their claims that there was a mass demand for keg beer and no demand at all for the traditional variety. The campaign tested the strength of a wide variety of beers and showed that the keg versions were nearly always both dearer and weaker than the real thing. They showed, too, that demand was created by expensive advertising and nurtured by the simple fact that in thousands of pubs they were the only beers available. According to one of its founder members, Graham Lees, CAMRA 'was born in an era of unfettered big business whizzkids whose ultimate strategy was a drinking Britain controlled by perhaps only three super breweries, owning all of the country's 60,000 pubs and each churning out a similar insipid bastardised beer'.

CAMRA was fortunate that it could argue its case in the open forum of the public house, where conversation naturally turns to discussing the merits of beer. Ever since the first Saxon ale house opened, drinkers have been moaning that 'beer isn't what it used to be'. At last something was being done about it. CAMRA created a climate in which further concentration of the brewing industry was politically unpopular. Smaller breweries that had toyed with the idea of going over to all-keg production or giving up brewing altogether discovered a growing market for their traditional ales. Beer festivals brought together traditional beers from all over Britain and drinkers discovered a profusion of tastes that came as a pleasant shock to palates atrophied by fizzy 'maltade'.

The Big Six hurried to mend their fences with the drinking

public. They produced new traditional beers or dusted off long forgotten ones. Handpumps sprouted on bars. Watney, which had earned the soubriquet 'Grotney' from CAMRA, had phased out all traditional beer in its headlong rush for keg promotion. But its replacement for Red Barrel, called simply Red, was not a success in spite of an enormous promotion. The group admitted that it had misread the market. There was a demand for regional beers as well as national keg brands, it agreed, and produced traditional ales again.

CAMRA's lasting achievement has been to show that when consumers band together and make a fuss then even giant multinationals have to listen. The concern for healthy living and better quality food has been made possible by a climate that CAMRA helped produce. What consumers cannot do, however, is to change the structure of an industry, especially one held in the sway of six giants. The big brewers made gestures to the real ale lobby and backed down from the promotion of their lacklustre keg bitters. But they began to manipulate the market in a new and highly profitable manner with lager. In 1971, lager accounted for just 7 per cent of beer production. Today it stands at more than 40 per cent. That jump has been achieved by some of the slickest and most expensive marketing in modern times. Its appeal is primarily to the young. Promotions suggest that unless you drink lager you are in some way odd, not a proper paid-up member of your peer group. If you want to be 'streetwise' and have credibility with the opposite sex then you must consume lager. It is a remarkable victory for marketing power, for here is a drink largely without a definable taste or character that within two decades has come from nowhere to challenge the supremacy of mild, bitter and stout. Above all, it is a drink that has made even greater fortunes for the brewing giants because of its profitability. The technical difference between beer and lager is explained in the next chapter. But most of the standard lagers brewed in Britain have little in common with the fine bottom-fermented beers of Europe. They are not stored or lagered for months in the correct fashion. They are thin and gassy. They are low in alcohol but priced at up to 10p a pint more than stronger bitters. As brewers pay less duty on weak beers, it is easy to see why lager is so profit-rich for the brewers.

Throughout the history of beer there have been changes in taste and demand. Sweet unhopped ale gave way to hopped beer. Dark, heavy porter was replaced by lighter pale ale or bitter. Those changes were determined by genuine consumer preference. It would be absurd to suggest that the rise of lager has been created solely by advertising, though the fact that the brewing industry spends 60 per cent of its advertising budget promoting lager shows how the consumer's elbow is effectively jogged. Lager is also part of a general and peculiar trend towards blandness in foodstuffs. Light white wines, homogenised and dosed with sulphur dioxide, are preferred to the robust palates of rich red wines. Instant coffee finds favour because of its lack of 'offensive' coffee taste. White bread with the texture of damp tissue paper is in far greater demand than chewy wholemeal. Traditional draught beer has become a drink for connoisseurs, for people who are not affronted by flavour.

The proponents of keg beers and lager argue that they are better because they are 'modern' and must necessarily be a sign of progress. In an astonishingly vituperative attack on the real beer movement in *Brewing Review* in 1986, Anna MacLeod, Professor of Brewing at Heriot-Watt University in Edinburgh, spoke of modern Luddites and 'muck and mystery merchants'. No doubt the same arguments are used against wine makers. After all, why bother to make champagne in its time-honoured traditional fashion when it is perfectly possible to make a sparkling wine in a large steel vat pumped full of carbon dioxide? Like lager and keg beers, all it lacks is flavour and that indefinable quality, character. The logic of the modernists is that we should exist on a diet of Pot Noodles, Mother's Pride and Harp lager.

In spite of CAMRA's success in creating interest in and demand for traditional draught beer, there are now new worrying economic trends in the brewing industry that once again threaten its survival. In 1986 the Australian combine Elders IXL bought the Courage brewing group. Elders owns Fosters lager, already sold throughout the Watney empire. Elders plans to sell Fosters in Courage pubs too. There have been rumours for several years that two American brewers, Anheuser-Busch (owners of Budweiser) and Miller, are keen to buy British breweries. The names of Watney and Scottish & Newcastle have been suggested as possible targets. This interest in Britain has been generated by the fact that many breweries are operating at less than full capacity. The slack could be taken up by brewing lager for export. The key to the conundrum lies in West Germany. In March 1987 the European Court decided that the Federal Republic's 'pure beer law', the *Reinheitsgebot*, was a restraint of trade because it prevented the import of other EEC countries' beers. The ruling means that beers brewed in France, Holland, Britain and other EEC countries using such unmalted ingredients as rice, corn starch and pasta flour and propped up by sulphites and other chemical aids can flood into Germany, the largest beer market in the world. Overseas companies that buy their way into the British 'beerage' will give short shrift to low volume, short-life traditional draught beer if it stands in the way of making a killing in Europe.

The trend towards 'Euro-beer' also threatens the existence of the British hop industry. Lager uses seedless, unfertilised hops. British beer is brewed from fertilised strains and has a higher hop rate. The number of British hop growers has halved since the early 1960s and the area under cultivation has slumped from 8,500 hectares to 4,700. Many British brewers prefer to use cheap seedless hops from Germany, Eastern Europe and even China. The gloomier hop growers believe that the British industry could disappear entirely by the end of the century, with a resulting change to the nature and taste of British beer.

In 1986 the government announced a two-year investigation of the tied house system by the Monopolies and Mergers Commission. It is likely that the commission will recommend at least that tenants of tied houses should have the right to buy some of their

CHAPTER NINE

Put the kettle on

From the barley and hop fields to the brewery: a step-by-step guide to brewing and the differences between traditional beer, keg and lager.

*Cornelius O'Sullivan, head brewer at Bass, Burton,
testing the quality of the King's Ale
brewed for the coronation of 1902.*

The way in which British beer is brewed is rather like making tea. In the north of England people speak of 'mashing' the tea and exactly the same expression is used when the barley malt is standing in its 'tea pot' – the mash tun. But before that stage of brewing is reached the raw barley has to be transformed into a soluble, sugar-rich material suitable for fermenting into alcohol. When barley is harvested the grains are rock hard and contain starch, not sugar. They are taken to the brewery or, more usually these days, to a specialist maltster. His task is to unlock the natural sugars. This is done by 'steeping', by placing the barley grains in large tanks of water. The barley soaks up the water and begins to sprout. Once germination is under way the grains are taken to a large room known as the malting floor where they are spread out and turned repeatedly by men with shovels. The grains are left to grow for up to eight days, by which time small shoots have broken through the husk of the grain. The process is slow, gentle and skilful. The maltster must use his judgement to decide when the starch has been converted and is ready to be turned into malt. He then transfers it to a kiln where the grains are heated by warm air to a temperature of about 60 degrees C, which stops germination. The heat is then adjusted according to the type of barley needed by the brewer. If he wants a pale malt then the temperature will be raised to around 80 degrees C. A darker beer needs darker malt, kilned at around 90 to 110 degrees C. Roasted barley for stout is kilned at a much higher temperature and is used mainly for adding colour and flavour as there is little fermentable content left. We now have malt. If you visit a brewery and are given some malt to eat it has a pleasant biscuity flavour and is now ready to be turned into beer.

By tradition, brewing begins early in the morning when sensible people are asleep or sleeping it off. In some breweries, the head brewer, a man held in great esteem, sits in a special chair and at the appointed hour, often 4am, gives the order to 'start the brew'. At this stage he needs malt and water. The malt has been stored in sacks and is now passed through sieves to remove any foreign bodies such as small stones or nails that came with the barley from the countryside. When the malt is clean it is poured into a mill and lightly crushed into a powder called grist which pours down a chute into a large container named the mash tun. Hot water or liquor floods into the tun at a temperature of 77 degrees C. The word water is never used in breweries perhaps for fear that it could be considered a comment on the finished product. It is stored in liquor tanks, usually at the top of the building. Even the strongest beers are made up of more than 90 per cent water and liquor is a vital ingredient. Whether it comes from the brewery's own wells or from the public supply, it is treated to ensure absolute purity and salts may be added to give it the degree of hardness needed for brewing pale ale.

The mash tun is filled almost to the top and the infusion of malt and liquor is left for two or three hours. If you cook porridge you will have seen how the oats swell and absorb the liquid. What happens in the mash tun is similar as the natural sugars in the malt dissolve into the thick porridgy liquid. When the brewer is satisfied that maximum conversion has taken place he opens the bottom of the mash tun, which has a slotted base. The sweet liquid is called wort and flows out of the vessel, leaving the porridgy mass of grains behind. Revolving arms in the roof of the mash tun now spray or sparge more hot liquor over the grains to wash out any remaining sugars that have been left behind. Brewing is full of curious old names such as wort, grist, mash and sparge. Many of them are of Saxon, old German or Dutch origin. In the Guinness breweries, mash tuns are called kieves, from an old French word *cuivre* or keep. The word quiver, the pouch in which archers keep their arrows, comes from the same source. The grains left behind in the mash tun are

The porridgy mixture of liquor and malt in a mash tun, with the sparging arms in the roof of the vessel.

shovelled out and sold as animal feed.

The sweet wort is pumped to a copper or brew kettle where it is heated to boiling point for one or two hours. Before the arrival of the hop, boiling was carried out to ensure that the liquid was free from dangerous bacteria but now the copper is the place where hops are added to give that essential bitterness to the finished beer. Hops are stored in sacks known as pockets that have little sticky-out ears at the corners. British brewers have for long favoured such home-grown varieties as Fuggles and Goldings but the influence of lager and the Common Market has seen a swing to European seedless hops and a new British variety called Target, which is cheaper to use because it is high in the essential alpha acid that gives the bitterness to beer. The brewer has to judge just how long to let boiling continue. If it goes on too long a degree of bitterness from the hops will be lost. Some brewers, courtesy of Mr Gladstone's change in the law in 1880, may add brewing sugar while the wort is being boiled to add to the sweetness but others prefer to rely solely on the natural sugars in the malt. When boiling is finished the hopped wort flows into another vessel called the hop back, which has a slotted base. The spent hops settle on the base and act as a filter as the liquid runs through. The hopped wort is cooled by running through a coiled refrigerator called a paraflow and then into the fermenting vessels. The large rooms in which fermentation takes place must be kept spotlessly clean to avoid any bacteria or wild yeasts ruining the beer.

Before fermentation can begin, the government steps in. In most countries, brewers pay excise duty on their beers when they are ready to leave the breweries. It is essential if genuine lager is being produced for it is often stored for several months and brewers would be penalised if they had to pay duty long before the beer was drunk. In Britain, again thanks to Mr Gladstone's changes of 1880, the duty is levied on the wort before it is fermented. An excise officer, who works full-time in many large breweries, assesses the 'original gravity' of the wort with a hydrometer, a measure of the sugars present in the liquid. Water has a gravity of 1000 degrees. If 40 parts of 'fermentable material' are added to water, the beer is said to have an original gravity of 1040 degrees. The strength of any particular beer will depend upon the amount of malt and sugar used. The weakest beers have gravities of around 1030 degrees, rare strong ones are as high as 1100. The average gravity of all the beers brewed in Britain today is 1037 degrees.

Now fermentation can take place and what happens next marks the great divide between the two basic styles of beer, British ale and the rest of the world's lager. The yeast used for British beer, *Saccharomyces cerevisiae*, is known as a top fermenting yeast because it works on top of the wort at a temperature of 15–20 degrees C. Yeast is made up of millions of tiny fungus cells that go beserk when they are confronted by a liquid rich in sugar. Some ten hours after the yeast has been poured into the fermenting vessel and thoroughly mixed with

Skimming the yeast: top fermentation creates a thick yeasty head.

the wort, a thick yellowy-white head builds up on top of the liquid. The head is formed by the carbon dioxide gas created as the yeast converts the sugars into alcohol. In some breweries the yeast head is roused with large wooden paddles to ensure that it is in contact with all the wort in the fermenter. Two days later the yeasty head is skimmed from the top of the wort, leaving sufficient yeast behind to continue fermentation. As yeast multiplies at such an enormous rate, there is never a shortage unless a brewery is unlucky enough to get a yeast infection, which means scrapping the batch and starting a new strain. That rarely happens these days and most strains are used for decades. The yeast strain used in the old Bass union room at Burton was more than 100 years old. The yeast that is skimmed from the wort is carefully squeezed and pressed into manageable proportions and kept in refrigerators. Excess yeast is sold to Marmite and other yeast extract firms.

About a week after fermentation began the alcohol starts to overpower the yeast, which sinks slowly to the bottom of the fermenter. We now have unfinished 'green' beer and it goes in different directions in the brewery. The beer destined to become keg or bottled is run into tanks where it is chilled and then filtered to remove all the yeast solids. It is then bottled or kegged under carbon dioxide pressure and pasteurised. Some beer that is kept in large cellar tanks in pubs or clubs with a quick turnover is not necessarily pasteurised and is known as 'bright' beer. All beers given some or all of these treatments are called 'brewery conditioned'. Whatever their protagonists may say, they lack the mature, rounded flavours of beer that is left to condition naturally. This type of beer, cask conditioned or 'real ale', is kept for a few days in conditioning tanks. The remaining yeast slowly continues to produce alcohol and carbon dioxide and purges the beer of harsh and unpleasant flavours. From the tanks the beer is run into casks through openings in the top known as the shive. Casks are made from wood or metal. The material has no effect on the final taste of the beer though some nostalgists believe that wood is best. A handful of hops to give aroma and liquid sugar to encourage a strong secondary fermentation are also added at this stage. A gooey substance called finings is put either into the cask or the conditioning tank to clear the beer. Both the shive and the bung hole at the end of the cask are sealed and the beer is ready for its last journey . . . to the pub cellar.

It is not yet ready to be drunk. The cask is set up on chocks in the cellar to keep it steady and a tap is knocked in through the bung hole. The shive on top has a soft core and this is removed and replaced by a soft wooden peg known as a spile. Inside the cask the beer continues to ferment vigorously and the carbon dioxide produced escapes through the spile. At the same time the finings are slowly dragging all the yeasty solids to the belly of the cask. After a day, the publican or his cellarman will replace the soft, porous spile with a harder one that stops the gas escaping. If all the gas left the cask the beer would be flat.

Depending on the beer – some are said to 'drop bright' faster than others – it is ready to be drunk within two or three days of arriving at the pub. When it is ready, the tap in the bung is connected to the beer line and the beer is drawn to the bar either by a manual pump or an electric one. The journey to the pub wasn't the beer's final journey. It now makes the pleasant trip down the drinker's throat. After all the effort, the mashing, the boiling, the heaving and frothing of fermentation and the slow ripening in the cask, you have natural British beer in all its glory and profusion of tastes.

The system outlined above is based on a traditional brewery where all the stages of producing beer are open to inspection. In some modern plants, new technology has been introduced. Mashing, boiling and fermenting times and temperatures are computerised and brewing goes on inside closed vessels. The staff follow its progress on a control panel. It does not mean that the finished product is better or worse than beer brewed in the traditional fashion but it is certainly less fun to watch. Beers can change their characters quite noticeably if the brewing method is altered. Draught Bass is a case in point. It was brewed in the union room at Burton and in spite of its quite high gravity of 1044 degrees it had a superb, delicate palate. Then in the early 1980s Bass closed the union room on the grounds of the cost of maintenance (probably a fraction of the money the company spends every year advertising Carling Black Label) and transferred production to modern enclosed conical fermenters. Draught Bass has never been the same since. It is a pleasant enough beer but it is heavy and slightly sweet, not a patch on a beer that was once justifiably promoted as 'the great ale of old England'.

In Scotland, as was noted in the chapter *Heavy going*, beer is fermented at a lower temperature than in England and Wales and has a longer conditioning time. When cask-conditioned beer reaches a pub cellar in Scotland it is not set up in the English style. The cask is upended and a long metal tube known as an extractor is inserted into the bung hole. The tube is joined to the air pressure system that delivers the beer to the bar. The advantage is that the casks take up less space in the cellar and, canny Scots, the beer can start to be served as soon as the beer begins to settle and clear from the top of the cask.

The styles of British beer fall into distinct categories:

MILD: Until the end of the Second World War, the British drank more mild than bitter. As it is a weaker drink, mild was cheaper and therefore popular with people on low incomes. Mild has gone out of fashion in many areas but is still popular in the Midlands, the North-West and Wales. It is usually dark in colour due to the use of darker malt or the addition of caramel. Superb examples include Ansells' mild in the West Midlands, Brain's Dark in Cardiff and Thwaite's mild from Blackburn. Not all mild is dark in colour, though. Several breweries produce light milds though the distinction between light mild and bitter is blurred. In Hertfordshire, McMullen brew a delectable light mild named AK. Nobody is sure why it is called by this name. I have heard claims that AK stands for 'Asquith's Knockout', a reference to a heavy increase in beer duty brought in by the Chancellor of the Exchequer during World War One. But the name AK was used by brewers long before that time. It is more likely that it was just a way of labelling the beer in the brewery. Worthington E, for example, is so called because Worthington brewed several bitters and labelled the casks A, B, C, D . . . and E. The original gravity of mild is usually around the 1031 to 1035 mark.

BITTER is Britain's most popular beer, a style famous throughout the world, the descendant of India Pale Ale. Its characteristic is its pale brown colour – though there are many coppery bitters – and high rate of hopping from which the name derives. There are bitters to suit all tastes, from the shocking hoppiness of Shepherd Neame's Master Brew, produced in the heart of the Kent hop fields at Faversham, the lighter, quenching bitters of the West Country, London's traditionally dry style personified by Young's 'Ordinary' bitter – a misnomer if ever there was one – to the sweeter bitters of the Midlands, the creamy brews of

Yorkshire and the sharp, distinctive style of the North-West and Wales. Gravities are of the 1035–1039 degrees level. BEST or SPECIAL BITTER indicates a stronger version that is probably closer to the original IPAs as they have gravities that range from the mid-1040s to the 1050s. They are fuller and slightly sweeter in taste. Bitters such as Ruddle's County, Greene King Abbot and Fuller's Extra Special Bitter are superb examples of the breed but they should be savoured in small quantities.

STOUT to most people is synonymous with Ireland but its origins are English. Porter was first brewed in London and its popularity was slow to spread across the Irish Sea. When it did take root there, though, it was never surpassed by pale ale. Arthur Guinness started in business in 1759 and forty years later he adapted his Dublin brewery to produce only porter and, later, the stronger extra stout. Porter lingered on in the north of Ireland until the 1970s but now Guinness brews only extra stout, though other forms are produced for export. Two smaller Irish brewers, Beamish & Crawford and Murphy, both from Cork, also brew stout and they have recently found small niches in the British market where stout is enjoying a small revival. The characteristic of stout, of course, is its jet black colour, formed by the use of roasted malts and roasted unmalted barley. Stout is generously hopped, which gives it a brilliant balance between bitterness and maltiness. The draught versions of the three Irish stouts are all pressurised but the pressure is low and does not make them unpleasantly fizzy. They have original gravities of around 1040.

Guinness Extra Stout in the bottle is an example of a rare and dying breed, a *naturally-conditioned* bottled beer. Before the tankers leave the Guinness brewery for the bottling plants, some partially fermented wort known as gyle beer is added. This starts to 'work' and when the beer is bottled it undergoes a secondary fermentation that creates a small sediment. Publicans have to rotate their stocks to make sure that each batch has reached its peak before it is served. Living Guinness is one of the finest beers in the world, rich, bitter-sweet and tangy, the carbonation produced naturally inside the bottle. Sadly, it is under threat. Already all bottled Guinness in Scottish pubs and in off-licences and supermarkets throughout Britain is now chilled, filtered and pasteurised, a beer quite different in taste and character. Guinness says it has no plans to phase out the living variety from pubs in England and Wales. Let us hope the company is true to its word. Unlike Guinness, which can be found in just about every pub in the land, Imperial Russian Stout is hard to find. It is brewed only occasionally and has to mature in oak casks for several months. Since the closure of the Courage brewery in London it is brewed by John Smiths of Tadcaster. Seek out this heavy, rich beer with a gravity of 1101 degrees and discover why it tickled the Tsarina's tastebuds.

Few breweries can be bothered to produce sediment bottle beers. Gale of Horndean in Hampshire do. Prize Old Ale is a fruity barley wine in a stoppered bottle and a powerful gravity of 1095 degrees. Next door in Dorset, Eldridge Pope of Dorchester pays homage to the literary giant of Wessex with nip bottles of Thomas Hardy's Ale. It has a gravity of 1125 degrees and is the strongest beer brewed regularly in Britain. The brewery recommends that you lay it down for several years until it reaches maturity. It is a frustrating business. You stare at the little bottle for years and when it is finally time to open it the contents disappear with one gulp. It is quite a gulp, though.

One bottle-conditioned beer that can be found widely in Bass group pubs and in some of its rivals' outlets too, is Worthington White Shield, the descendant of the original India Pale Ale. There is a considerable mystique attached to the way in which this strong, nutty, 1052 gravity beer is poured. If you do it properly in the brewery, Bass will give you a certificate of worthiness. The rules are as follows. Remove the cap and let the beer stand for a minute or two (this is the first test of the drinker's dedication) to allow some of the natural carbonation to work itself off. Then raise bottle and glass to eye level, holding the glass almost horizontal. Bring the bottle towards the glass but do not let it touch the rim – this is considered to be cheating.

Ale of Casterbridge: a bottle of Thomas Hardy's Ale and a letter from the author to the brewers, Eldridge Pope, in a recreation of Hardy's study in the Dorchester Museum.

As you can see, you need steady hands and nerves to carry out this delicate operation. Start to pour slowly. Don't rush or you will build up too much head of foam and you will not get all the beer into the glass. Raise the glass as it fills and at the same time watch the sediment begin to move down the bottle towards the neck. Just as the sediment reaches the end of the neck, stop pouring and you should have a glass of crystal clear beer. White Shield is in perfect drinking condition one month after it leaves the brewery. There is no need to throw away the sediment. Keen home brewers can use it to ferment their beers. I am told that it kills slugs. Some perverse drinkers, when they have finished the glass of beer, pick up the bottle and empty the sediment down their throats. It does you no harm but it can give you a bad case of the 'trots'.

107

Many breweries brew draught versions of strong OLD ALES or BARLEY WINES. They have gravities ranging from 1050 to 1090 degrees and are usually brewed for the winter months and a small glass is ideal for keeping the cold from your bones. They go under a variety of names – Old Ale, Christmas Ale or Winter Warmer – and are often poured straight from small casks called pins kept on the pub bar.

The British used to be great mixers of beer. When I was young I heard people order such concoctions as 'brown and mild', 'old and mild' and 'mild and bitter'. The habit seems to be declining though in London many drinkers still call for a 'light and bitter'. It seems an odd preference, for you are mixing the bottled version of bitter: pale ale is bottled best or special bitter, while light ale is ordinary bitter in bottled form. The rich used to mix (and may still do so for all I know) Guinness and champagne to make Black Velvet. Guinness and bitter mixed is a Black and Tan. People sensitive to Irish history should avoid it. And history aside, why spoil perfection?

A common misconception is that British beer is warm. It is certainly brewed to be served at a higher temperature than lager but that does not mean it should be served at room temperature. Whatever its attributes, British beer is not claret and does not have to be *chambré*. The ideal cellar temperature is 14 degrees C (57 degrees F). The beer in your glass should be pleasantly cool and refreshing. If it is warm, tell the landlord. He will either change the beer or throw you out. It is a risky business.

Finally, a few words about LAGER. For centuries all beer was brewed using top fermenting yeasts. The problem was that in countries with hot climates the beer was often sour and unpleasant. It was found that if the beer was fermented and conditioned in deep caves packed with natural ice it did not go sour. The yeast settled to the floor of the fermenter and did not create a thick head that needed to be skimmed. This style of brewing was mentioned in Munich early in the 15th century. Gradually a new strain of bottom-fermenting yeast was developed. With the industrial revolution and refrigeration, lager beer (lager is the German word for 'store') created a world-wide demand. Jacob Christiansen Jacobsen, the owner of the Carlsberg brewery in Denmark, made a long and arduous journey to Munich in 1845 to bring back two quarts of Bavarian yeast. On the return journey, he stopped the coach frequently to cool the pots in water to prevent the precious yeast from going off. As a result of his scientific work on yeast culture, bottom-fermenting yeast was named *Saccharomyces carlsbergensis* in his honour, though more recently the name has been changed to *Saccharomyces uvarum*.

Lager beer is brewed today using pale malts (though there are some dark lagers) and seedless hops as well as lager yeast. The mashing system is the decoction form not the infusion mash used in Britain. It starts at a lower temperature of 35 degrees C and lasts much longer. Sections of the mash are removed from the tun, heated to a higher temperature and returned. The aim is to achieve a greater conversion of the sugars. The wort is not filtered in the mash tun but is transferred to another vessel known as a lauter tun. When it has been boiled with hops and cooled the wort undergoes primary fermentation at 7 to 12 degrees C. Primary fermentation lasts for one or even two weeks and only a slight yeast scum can be seen on the surface of the wort. The beer is transferred to conditioning tanks and kept at a temperature of freezing point or very slightly higher. This is the lagering or secondary fermentation stage, with the yeast continuing to change the remaining sugars into alcohol. Small amounts of partially fermented wort can be added – a system known as 'krausening'. Lagering lasts for four or five weeks, though some stronger European beers are stored for nine months or more. Lager is traditionally stronger than British beer. Even standard lager beers have gravities in the mid-1040s. European brewers say it is impossible to get a true, rounded lager taste below 1040 degrees. They are helped by the fact that excise duty is much lower in the rest of Europe than in Britain and Ireland. In Britain most standard lagers have gravities in the mid-1030s. They are based loosely on the Pilsener style which originated in

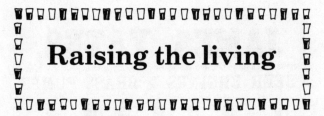

CHAPTER TEN

Raising the living

The large modern public house needed quicker service than pot boys running up and down to the cellar with jugs of beer. The 19th century saw the development of the 'beer engine' triggered by a handpump on the bar to pull beer from the cask.

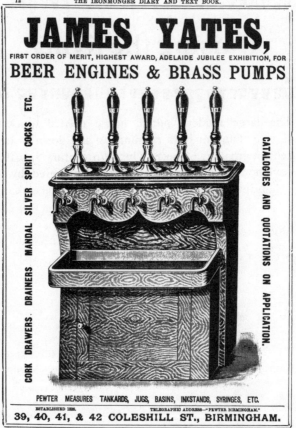

JAMES YATES,

FIRST ORDER OF MERIT, HIGHEST AWARD, ADELAIDE JUBILEE EXHIBITION, FOR

BEER ENGINES & BRASS PUMPS

CORK DRAWERS. DRAINERS MANDAL SILVER SPIRIT COCKS ETC.

CATALOGUES AND QUOTATIONS ON APPLICATION.

PEWTER MEASURES TANKARDS, JUGS, BASINS, INKSTANDS, SYRINGES, ETC.

ESTABLISHED 1826.   TELEGRAPHIC ADDRESS—"PEWTER BIRMINGHAM."

39, 40, 41, & 42 COLESHILL ST., BIRMINGHAM.

Victorian advertisement for a bank of beer engines.

If British beer is unique then so are the methods used for serving it. The best-known English system, the beer engine operated by a handpump on the bar, once travelled widely to help serve cask-conditioned beer throughout the colonies. But as the world lager revolution spread, cask beer and its engines became confined to their country of origin. The beer engine arrived on the pub scene early in the 19th century. It coincided with and was prompted by the decline of the publican brewer and the rise of the commercial companies that began to dominate the supply of beer to public houses. The common brewers expected a healthy return on the sales of their products. They also wanted the beer to be stored and served in exemplary condition in the pubs they supplied. And as the brewers' profits grew and beer prices rose, the publicans found that their margins were being squeezed. In order to sell more beer and maintain their livings, publicans looked for faster and less labour-intensive methods of serving beer.

In *The Brewing Industry in England, 1700–1830*, Peter Mathias records that 'most beer had to be stored in butts in the publicans' cellars for the technical reason that it needed an even and fairly low temperature, even where convenience and restricted space behind the bar did not enforce it. This meant, equally inevitably, continuous journeying to and from the cellars by the pot-boys to fill up jugs from the spigots: a waste of time for the customer and of labour and trade for the publican. Drawing up beer from the cellar at the pull of a handle at the bar at once increased the speed of sale and cut the wage bill.'

The first person to attempt to invent a system for raising beer from cellar to bar was Joseph Bramah who took out a patent for a beer pump in October 1797. Bramah had successfully patented such socially useful devices as the hydraulic press and an improved water closet, but his beer engine created as many problems as it sought to solve. Specifications for Bramah's pump show a man at ground level filling a jug with beer from a pipe that leads to storage vessels below the ground. The pipe ends in a tap and the beer was to be drawn from the cellar by an elaborate system of heavy boxes of sand raised on pistons that fitted into voluminous storage containers. As the boxes pressed down on the beer in the containers it forced it through pipes up to the bar. This system of 'sand pressure' had obvious drawbacks: it required cellars with considerable height to accommodate the containers and pistons, while normal butts or casks delivered by the breweries were not suitable as they did not have vertical sides. Publicans would have had to transfer beer from butts to the new containers, activity that would have been as troublesome and labour-intensive as fetching beer from the cellar in jugs. Bramah's invention did not get out of the cellar let alone off the ground. But his idea encouraged others to find a solution to the problem, though Mathias wondered why it had taken so long to be invented: 'One of the few technical devices of importance to come into it [the public house] since the publican stopped brewing his own beer was the beer engine. It was, from the first, a simple manually-operated pump, incorporating no advances in hydraulic knowledge or engineering skill, similar in design to many pumps used at sea, yet perfectly adapted to its function in the public house. It was brought into this environment by the need for speed and efficiency caused by the intensive demand in a busy city tavern. One wonders why such a thing had not been used before, particularly in ports where seamen, all too familiar with pumps, often became publicans; or even more where brewers, who used many pumps about their breweries, themselves controlled public houses.'

By 1801, John Chadwell of Blackfriars Road, London, was registered as a 'beer-engine maker' and soon afterwards Thomas Rowntree in the same area described himself as 'a maker of a double-acting beer-machine'. A.G. Green, again in the Blackfriars region of London, was similarly registered by 1809 and it is likely that the 'patent brewing-machine warehouse' of Needham, Rawlings and Co was engaged in the same manufacture. Yates and Greenaway were also early beer engine manufacturers. In his *Treatise on Mechanics*, published in 1806, Olinthus Gregory referred in passing to 'beer-drawing machines – nothing else than an assemblage of small pumps, either sucking or forcing.' A 'patent beer engine' was among the fittings offered for sale with a public house in 1801 and one with 'four motions' was sold in 1806. In 1812 a valuation of the equipment in the Crown in Fleet Street listed a 'three-motion' beer engine with 'Pewter Sink, Lead Pipe, Screw Cocks and apparatus complete, fixed in a neat, inlaid Mahogany Case'. By this time trade directories in other major English cities such as Bristol and Birmingham were listing beer engine makers. The *Pantalogia* of 1813 reported that such machines were 'very common in London and other large towns'. One had been installed in a rural pub in Tewin in Hertfordshire as early as 1806. Peter Mathias commented sourly: 'Considering its rapid adoption at the turn of the century, encouraged then, no doubt, by the profit margins of publicans falling as prices rose, we may perhaps think that the device had been held up so long only by an instinctive conservatism and an irrational conviction that pumps were only for water, that engines pumping beer savoured of fountains flowing with wine – fictions fit only for continental extravagance.'

There is no recorded evidence of consumer objection to the beer engine. At a time when public houses were open for long periods and demand for beer was insatiable, customers seemed to value a system that served their drinks quickly and refreshingly cool. By the 1820s, beer engine service had become standard throughout most of urban England and Gaskell and Chambers, the world-renowned makers of drink dispensing equipment, had taken the lead in their manufacture. Such was the demand for engines that during Victorian times Gaskells had more than 700 employed in their Birmingham works alone. By the end of the century some vast London and other big city taverns had banks of 40 to 50 handpumps pulling and heaving to meet the demand for beer. Because of the effort involved a popular form of beer engine was the 'cash register' variety, a bank of three or four pumps mounted with short handles high on the bar, which needed less physical strength to operate them. The George in Southwark, South London, still has a 144 year-old working cash register engine.

The earliest system of engine survived until as late as the 1940s. This comprised lead pipes connected to the casks in the cellar and to a 'leather-bucket' engine below the bar. As early as 1795 Sir George Baker had shown that the illness known as 'Devonshire colic' was in reality lead poisoning, but lead pipes continued to be used in beer engines until well into the 20th century, when their use was banned by law. They were replaced first by porcelain or glass pipe sections about four inches in length, interconnected by rubber tubes. They were followed by stainless steel pipes and today the universal type of piping is micro-bore plastic. Leather bucket engines also disappeared, giving way to all-metal piston engines. In the late 1970s the possibility of EEC legislation prompted brewers and engine manufacturers to replace gunmetal working parts with stainless steel or plastic. The modern beer engine is a perfectly safe method of serving beer if all the working parts and the pipes are cleaned regularly. Some brewery companies – Banks and Hansons of the West Midlands are the best-known examples – prefer, however, to serve their cask beers by electric pumps.

It was a similar and possibly misplaced concern for hygiene that prompted the introduction of the electric pump in the 1930s. It does exactly the same job as a manual engine but without the effort. It comes in two versions – the free-flow pump, which draws the beer until the tap on the bar is switched off, and the metered pump with a diaphragm that moves to and fro inside the mounting on the bar, measuring precise half pints. Electric pumps are rare in the south of England, widespread in the Midlands and often found in Wales and the north. The only possible objections to them are that they lack the aesthetic appeal of a tall handpump and that it is difficult, sometimes impossible

116

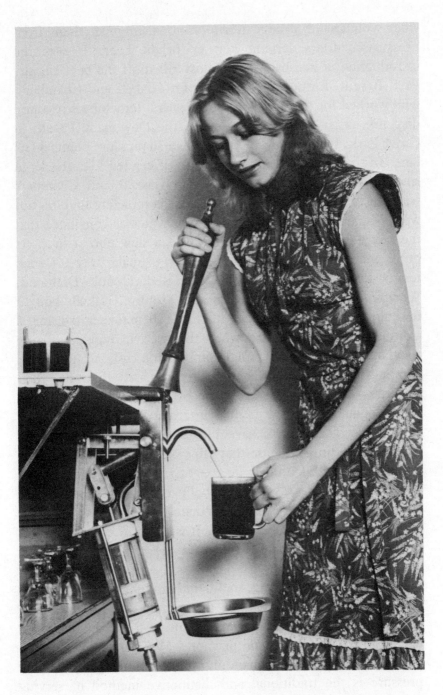

Handpump operating the suction pump of a beer engine.

when you are in strange territory, to distinguish them from pressurised fonts serving keg or bright beer. It was the introduction of keg beer that almost killed off the beer engine. Fred Bryant, former sales director for Gaskell and Chambers, who worked for the company for 43 years, remembers pressure dispense as far back as 1934, when the Downham Tavern in Grove Park, London, had no fewer than 30 pressure points on its bars. In the post-war years the spread of keg led to cutbacks in traditional beer engine manufacture. Gaskell and Chambers were on the point of phasing them out completely in 1966 but were persuaded not to by Fred Bryant who was convinced that the keg tide would turn. The tide was a slow ebb at first. As publicans discarded their beer engines to make way for such tongue-tingling delights as Watney's Red, Double Diamond, Worthington E, Tartan, Tavern and Trophy, Gaskells bought the engines for 2s 6d each and either sold them for scrap or for £6 a piece to the United States, where they were in demand as lamp standards. Today a new, single-pull engine costs around £120. Although Gaskell and Chambers have ceased to trade, their legendary Dalex engines are made by another firm and are in great demand, built by craftsmen from 70 year-old moulds. Firms such as Homark have introduced simplified styles of engine, including the type that clips on to the bar, which has found favour with landlords keen to experiment with real ale but not so keen to saw away a substantial part of their counter. In its various guises, the beer engine remains the rock on which the real ale revolution has been built. It is the symbol of all that is best in English and Welsh beer and the enduring sign of its quality and tradition.

The difference in serving traditional draught beer in Scotland is even more marked than the tastes and names of the beers themselves. Although beer engines can be found in some bars and Scottish and Newcastle promotes McEwan's cask beer on posters with a picture a handpump, the tall font primed by air pressure is the traditional and distinctive method of serving Scottish beer. The water engine arrived in the 1870s as the

Scottish brewing industry grappled with the same problem as the English one: how to keep and serve beer in the best condition. Ballinghall of Dundee was the first company to use air pressure and its original water engines were designed to produce pressures ranging from 121 lbs per square inch to 40 lbs per square inch. Other firms that moved quickly into water engine production were John McGlashan and Co, Gaskell and Chambers (Scotland) and Laidlaw and Sons. Aitkens of Edinburgh produced an engine and another was manufactured by Allan and Bogle of Glasgow. Two small engines, with the splendid names of Big Wonder and Little Wonder, were built in the United States and exported to Scotland, mainly for the Aberdeen area.

These engines were all similar in concept, a lavatory cistern in reverse, with water pressure being converted into air pressure. As water enters the casing or cistern, it raises a ball-cock and forces air through a float chamber to the air pipe connected to the cask, the process aided by an aptly-named snifter valve. The process is repeated until the required air pressure in the cask drives the beer to the bar. Water engines are now rare and have been replaced by electric air compressors, though many bars keep water engines in reserve in case of a power cut.

The other end of the system, the tall font on the bar, meets the requirements of ancient Scottish legislation that beer should be served in full view of the customer. The most distinctive and handsome font is the McGlashan Albany, still used to serve Maclay's cask beer. The font has a two-way tap. When the tap is operated it draws beer direct from the cask and any beer that overflows the glass goes into a return tray and is served through a second beer line when the tap is moved in the opposite direction. Many bars use a Cornelius font, originally designed for use with gas pressure systems of dispense but now widely used for cask beer too. As with the electric pump in England and Wales, it is not always possible to detect whether a Cornelius font is serving the real or the dead McCoy. If you don't like to ask then you have to pay your money and let your tastebuds do the rest. If they are immediately atrophied by Arctic bubbles then you

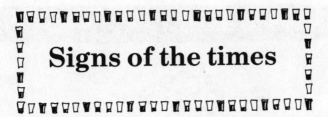

Signs of the times

Inn signs showed a mainly illiterate nation where ale, victuals and beds were available. Early signs were based on religious terms or used heraldic devices from the nobility. Trades people also had inns and taverns named after their company seals. Kings, queens, politicians and sportsmen have been honoured over the centuries.

Sign of the sexist times: pub sign based on a drawing by Hogarth.

The pub has a powerful influence on all our lives, even those sad souls who never set foot inside one. Long before the law allowed me to enter licensed premises, much of my time was spent on bus routes dotted with stops and fare stages named the Crooked Billet, the Green Gate, the Princess Alice, the Abbey Arms and the Boleyn. When education gave way to employment I travelled to Fleet Street by Underground, booking a ticket to a station named Blackfriars. Years later work took me further south across the Thames to London's most famous pub-cum-station, the Elephant and Castle. The benign influence has never waned and today the Green Line bus drops me in down-town St Albans at a stop known as the Rats Castle. Until my interest in beer and pubs developed naturally into a fascination with pub signs, I never paused to question why London Transport bus and train routes were dotted with such strange names. Like most people, even the most dedicated pub users, I did not realise that centuries of social history were encapsulated in the inn signs hanging over my head.

The bus stops of my schooldays show the influence that rural England, the church and the monarchy exercised over taverns and inns. Landlords who could not afford an elaborate painted sign made do with a simple log of twisted wood – a crooked billet. A green gate probably marked the spot where travellers paused to pay a toll, a natural place for a roadside inn to be built. The Abbey Arms may once have stood in the shadow of a religious house and dutifully portrayed the crest of the abbot. Princess Alice is a comparatively recent sign that pays respectful homage to a minor member of the Victorian royal family. The Boleyn stands in memory of the hapless Anne, who is reputed to have lived where West Ham football ground now stands at

123

Upton Park, East London. Purists will argue that Blackfriars, close to Fleet Street, takes its name from the monastic order that once lived and boozed there. But for most of us who know the area the history has been augmented by the remarkable Black Friar public house, turn-of-the-century art nouveau, a wedge-shaped frolic with coloured marble tops and carvings of toping friars at every turn. The Elephant and Castle may owe its name to the inability of the English to master foreign languages. Edward I's bride was a Spanish princess, the Infanta de Castillia, who lived for a time in south London. Elephant and Castle was the best the locals could manage. An alternative suggestion is that the area was named after a Spanish boat called the Infanta de Castillia that was moored in the Thames, but it is an implausible reason. The Elephant and Castle is a good mile or more from the river, a significant distance in a period when people either walked or went by horse-drawn transport. The most likely explanation, however, has nothing to do with Spanish princesses. The sign of the ancient Cutlers' Company was an elephant with a castle on its back.

The Rats Castle has no pretensions to history or royal connections. It is a unique name – many towns and cities have one such pub with an obscure and singular name – and in this case marks the spot where an earlier house became derelict and over-run with rats. The name is as simple as that, though no doubt in a hundred years' time more elaborate reasons will have been devised. That is the problem with a subject such as inn signs: once it becomes a popular hobby and weighty books are devoted to it, names thought up by god-fearing rural people and medieval craftsmen tend to be overlaid with plausible but dubious hindsight. Bag o' Nails, for example, is often said to be a corruption of Bacchanales, a boisterous celebration dedicated to Bacchus. It is just as likely that the name stems from drinking places used by carpenters. Pig and Whistle has suffered a similar fate, perhaps because it has acquired a curious popularity with writers and comedians, even though only a handful of pubs bear the name. Pig, we are told, comes from the Anglo-Saxon practice of marking drinking vessels with pegs to show how much had been consumed, while whistle is *wassail*, the Anglo-Saxon version of Bacchanales. Another school of thought suggests that pig is a corruption of the Anglo-Saxon *pightle*, meaning meeting place. All of this learned linguistics ignores the fact that a pig playing a whistle was a common pictorial feature of church architecture: a stall in Winchester cathedral, for example, shows a sow tootling on a flute.

Signs and crests were widespread in this country at a time when most of the populace was illiterate and there was no national let alone written language. Just as a lord's coat of arms on his military shields was the rallying point for his troops, so an inn sign showed the traveller or toiling labourer where they could pause for refreshment. A church carving of a pig and whistle is certain to have had more meaning for the common people than pightles and wassails.

Excavations at Pompeii revealed a number of shop signs, including the chequer board, the emblem of inn keepers who also acted as moneylenders: the boards used for playing chequers or draughts were also useful for piling coins of different denominations. The Romans brought the chequer board sign with them to Britain and it is still a popular pub name to the extent that one large brewing company, Watney's Wilson subsidiary in Manchester, uses it as a trade mark. The Romans also brought with them the habit of displaying a bunch of vine leaves to show that a taberna offered drink, food and accommodation. Not to be outdone, the ale-drinking natives developed the system of the ale stake, a long pole with a bunch of evergreens that protruded from simple roadside dwellings to indicate that freshly-brewed ale was available. Many brewers still hang a garland of flowers and evergreens outside a new pub and the names the Bush or Hollybush further commemorate the oldest and simplest of inn signs. Two further signs that pre-date Christianity are the Green Man and the Black Horse. The green or wild man – 'wodyn man' – is a reference to the pagan men who covered themselves in greenery and attacked travellers and

Ale stake, the earliest known form of tavern sign indicating that the ale wife had prepared a new brew.

sometimes whole villages. (Pubs called the Green Man but whose signs show Robin Hood are several centuries adrift.) Law-abiding citizens who tried to keep the highways safe from marauders rode black horses with muffled hooves.

The dreadful lawlessness of the country in the centuries that followed the departure of the Romans gave taverns and inns a special significance. Although many travellers no doubt had their throats cut and money stolen in ale houses, they were in general recognised as places of comparative safety. In 1393 Richard II introduced legislation that impelled landlords to erect signs to show that they offered sanctuary as well as board and lodging. The monarch was also mindful of the importance of the staple beverage of the inns, for the law stipulated that 'whosoever shall brew ale in the town with intention of selling it must hang out a sign, otherwise he shall forfeit his ale'. While only inns were forced by law to display signs, other trades people followed suit and soon whole streets of towns and cities were festooned with colourful signs to indicate the presence of bakers, cobblers, wig-makers, surgeons, corn chandlers and grocers. Landlords who were anxious that their houses should stand out prominently went to greater and absurder lengths to produce the most elaborate signs. The gallows sign stretching across the road became a popular feature until some became so heavy and ornate that they crashed to the ground, killing or injuring passers-by.

The most famous gallows sign, built for the White Hart at Scole in Norfolk in the 17th century, cost the staggering sum for the time of £1,000. Its artefacts included Jonah emerging from the whale's mouth, Neptune on a dolphin and an astronomer 'seated on a circumferenter and by some chymical preparations is so affected that in fine weather he faces that quarter from which it is about to come'. The White Hart is still a busy and thriving pub but its sign is no more. In spite of its great size, it simply disappeared or fell on to the back of a lorry.

The proximity of trades people to inns meant that they often used them for business as well as refreshment. The arms and crests of the various trade associations made splendidly colourful signs: the Bakers Arms, the Dolphin (watermen), Lamb and Flag (merchant tailors), Three Compasses (carpenters), Three Tuns (vintners), the Sugar Loaf (grocers), Noah's Ark (shipwrights) and Ram or Fleece (wool trade). But long before the development of trade, guilds and crafts, the older feudal influences of the church and nobility had made themselves felt. Some of the earliest inns were hostels for pilgrims that were attached to religious houses and supplied with ale brewed by the monks. The New Inn, possibly a corruption of Our Lady's Inn, was often the name given to accommodation built alongside churches and monasteries. The Crossed Keys, another popular old name, was the insignia of St Peter. The Mitre crops up frequently in cathedral cities, while the Lamb is a reference to Christ. The Bell, Five Bells and Eight Bells got their names from the number of bells in nearby churches. While many pubs called the Bull depict the animal, the original source is thought to be the *bulla* or *la boule*, the seal of a monastic order. The still popular Hope and Anchor, Anchor and Hope or just plain Anchor have religious not maritime connections: St Paul described hope 'as the anchor of the soul'.

Political pressure intervened to change some inn signs. When Henry VIII broke with Rome, landlords thought it discreet to change the Pope's Head to the King's Head. Popery in all its manifestations went out of the church window in Cromwell's time. The main sufferers were inns called the Angel or the Salutation, references to the annunciation of the Virgin Mary. In puritan times they were renamed either the Soldier and Citizen or, more vulgarly, the Flower Pot. Opponents of puritanism got their own back by corrupting God Encompasses Us to Goat and Compasses. Fervour for the religious crusades was marked by such names as the Turk's Head, Saracen's Head and – one of the oldest inns in England – the Trip to Jerusalem in Nottingham. Saints, too, were hung for posterity, the most popular by far being St George, the patron saint of England. He lost his sainthood under Cromwell, which explains the presence today of many pubs named simply the George.

Landlords often felt that it was politic to identify with the reigning monarch, hence the profusion of King's and Queen's Heads or Arms, the latter being a reference to their crests not their limbs. Crown or Rose and Crown are the most popular pub signs today. The rose celebrates the end of the long and bloody struggle between the houses of York and Lancaster. The heraldic signs of the royal and noble families naturally found favour with landlords anxious to tug an obsequious forelock, though they were quick to latch on to any change in political fortune. When Richard III, that most maligned of monarchs, met his death in Bosworth Field, there was an indecent rush to paint White Boars (his crest) blue. The Blue Boar was the badge of the Earl of Oxford, a supporter of Henry Tudor. Other heraldic inn signs still popular today include the Red Lion, the crest of John of Gaunt, the Bear and Ragged Staff of the Earls of Warwick, the White Bear (Kent), Green Dragon (Pembroke), Talbot, an extinct hunting dog (Shewsbury), Eagle (Cambridge), the White Horse (Arundel) and the Eagle and Child (Stanley, earls of Derby). The last and most unusual comes from a legend that a member of the Latham family of Lancashire, which married into the Stanley family, adopted a child found in an eagle's nest.

Travel down the centuries has been marked by the Pack Horse, the Coach and Horses, the Railway Tavern, the Ship, the

128

Clipper and more recently the Comet and the Double-O-Two. Animals and birds abound, from the Antelope to the Wolf, from the Blackbird to the Woodpecker, though many of these derive from heraldic symbols. The Swan with Two Necks (some pubs called this have signs showing a two-headed bird) is a corruption of Swan with Two Nicks. Swans had nicks or incisions made in their necks to indicate their ownership.

The Cat and Fiddle is said to be based on the exploits of an Englishman named Caton who held the port of Calais for a period during the Hundred Years War and was dubbed by the awed French *Caton le Fidèle* (Caton the Faithful). Another version suggests the name is a corruption of Catherina Fidelis, Catherine of Aragon. Both versions are about as likely as the Anglo-Saxon origins of Pig and Whistle.

Sport, if you are willing to accept blood sports as such, are celebrated by a variety of Fox and Hounds and a few Fighting Cocks and Game Cocks. One of the oldest licensed premises in England is Ye Olde Fighting Cocks in St Albans. Bear and bull baiting are recalled by the Bear and the Bull Ring. There are many Fishermen and Jolly Anglers while horse racing has its Starting Gates, Jockey and Gold Cup as well as several named after famous horses. The Bat and Ball at Hambledon, the Hampshire home of cricket, is just one of hundreds that mark the summer game; there is a profusion of Cricketers and W.G. Grace's hairy visage adorns the Yorker in London's Piccadilly. Association football is perhaps too modern a game to have inspired many names: there are a few dedicated to teams (the Gunners, the Spurs, the Hammers, the Saints and, inevitably, United). There is even an Alf Ramsey, though there are no plans similarly to honour later England managers.

Most inn and pub signs are curiously sedate and sober: jollity is reserved for the insides of the buildings. The Load of Mischief, a man forced to carry a nagging wife on his back – an original painting by Hogarth – and the Silent Woman, showing a headless lady, will find little favour these days. Some humour stems from poor workmanship. When the Rose was badly

129

painted it was nicknamed the Cauliflower. A similar fate befell vulgar versions of the Star and Garter, a leg in court dress wearing the jewelled emblem. They became known as the Haunch of Venison or the Leg of Mutton. They should not be confused with the Sir Loin of Beef. A pub in Chingford of that name used to have a splendid sign showing James I knighting a piece of meat. One of Watney's less recorded crimes is to have removed the sign and replaced it with a quite meaningless one that merely shows the king's head.

Not all pubs have names. In the early 19th century an unofficial drinking place called the Brace existed in the King's Bench court in London. Prisoners awaiting trial bought ale from two brothers named Partridge (hence the name of the place) who fetched drink from the pub next door and no doubt marked up the prices for the benefit of customers who had no opportunity to go elsewhere. It was an early example of a tied house.

Whatever the name and whatever its history, a pub sign should be one of welcome and good cheer. Republicans can rest content in the Queen's Arms, socialists can imbibe without fear in the Winston Churchill and Tories likewise in the Clement Attlee. Only one known hostelry spoils the image of warmth and friendship. For many years a bar in Glencoe bore a simple sign: No Campbells.

CHAPTER TWELVE

Haven't you got homes to go to?

Abbots moaned about monks drinking too much and inns had to close at curfew: from the earliest days of the ale house, the authorities have tried – often without success – to curb drinking. Thanks to David Lloyd George and the Defence of the Realm Act, the English and Welsh are still saddled with pub hours introduced in World War One.

In 745 AD the Archbishop of York declared that 'No priest go to eat or drink in taverns'. It is one of the earliest recorded examples of an attempt to prevent people from going to their local. It does not seem to have been successful. During the reign of Edgar, King of All England (959–975), the Archbishop of Canterbury, Dunstan, issued a canon that 'No priest to be an ale-scop [reciter], nor in any wise act the gleeman'. A gleeman, it is safe to assume, was a cheerful fellow who encouraged others to carouse. Edgar was also concerned by the scale of ale consumption and decreed that there should be only one ale house for each village. In the centuries that followed the church and state attempted to control drinking through curbs on opening times for outlets and taxes on ale and beer. Legislation has always been followed by ingenious attempts to get round the law, as we saw with the drinkers who decamped to the forests to enjoy their 'scot ales' in unlicensed premises. The Assize of Bread and Ale in the 13th century brought in both the ale conner or taster to judge the quality of ale and also stamped, measured containers to drink from. The courts were kept busy as a result, prosecuting brewers and brewsters who refused to entertain the ale conner, who sold ale in short measure and who did not exhibit a pole to show that a new brew had been made.

The 14th century saw the first attempts to curb the hours of inns and taverns. A proclamation issued in London in 1329 announced 'Whereas misdoers, going about by night, have their resort more in taverns than elsewhere, and there seek refuge and watch their hour for misdoing, we forbid that any taverner or brewer keep the door of his tavern open after the hour of curfew'. A similar proclamation in Bristol laid down that 'No taverner of wine or ale keep any guests sitting in their taverns

133

after the hour of curfew has rung, but shall immediately close their doors'. A century later ale house keepers in London and other cities were forbidden to sell ale on Sundays until High Mass had ended. Inns, a better class of establishment, were excluded from the requirement. In 1495 an Act of Parliament gave powers to justices of the peace 'to reject and put away Common ale-selling in towns and places where they should think convenient and to take sureties of keepers of ale houses in their good behaviour'. The act was consolidated in 1552 when ale house keepers were required to obtain licences from justices, a system that has prevailed to this day with a few minor breaks and hiccoughs. Inns and taverns were brought into line a few years later.

As well as knighting a loin of beef, James I was much exercised by the problem of immoderate behaviour in licensed premises. Acts of 1604 and 1606 attempted to tackle drunkenness. They were unsuccessful, for a further act of 1609 declared 'Notwithstanding all former laws and provisions already made, the inordinate and extreme vice of excessive drinking and drunkenness doth more and more abound'. The new act included powers to deprive retailers of their licences if they failed to keep orderly conduct in their houses. The law was renewed in 1623 and had clearly failed to curb the problem. James I's son, Charles I, was the first monarch to attempt to impose direct taxes on beer. He inherited a near-bankrupt economy and saw beer as a convenient milch-cow, rather in the style of modern Chancellors of the Exchequer. The king decided to levy a tax on brewers but this was an almost impossible task as every publican was also a brewer and there were more than 20,000 ale houses, taverns and inns in England and Wales alone. Charles decreed therefore that retailers of beer could only obtain their supplies from common or commercial brewers, a step that hastened the rise of a commercial brewing establishment and prompted the demise of publican brewers. When the civil war broke out (not over this issue) both king and parliament levied 'temporary' duty on brewing to help pay for the war effort. As with later temporary measures, duty has been with us ever since.

The 18th century was devoted mainly to attempting to curb the wild excesses of gin drinking but legislation also had an impact on retailers of beer. In 1710 all licensed victuallers were required to pay one shilling a year to renew their licences. In 1756 payment increased sharply to one guinea and a further ten shillings were added in 1784. These may seem trifling sums but they were quite substantial at a time when beer cost the customer a penny or two. A publican brewer also had to pay a brewing licence fee based on a sliding scale that began with a thousand barrels a year, a figure that covered most common brewers of the day. The licence at that level was thirty shillings a year. The sums of money involved encouraged more publicans to give up brewing and to take their supplies from the commercial firms.

The 19th century saw considerable upheaval in the retail trade as legislation piled on legislation. The Ale House Act of 1828 gave justices control over issuing licences to publicans, who could be prosecuted if they breached the law. Its direct opposite, the disastrous Beerhouse Act of 1830, took power away from the justices in the belief, probably quite justified, that the relationship between publicans and magistrates was often corrupt and that licences were too often granted in return for 'back-handers'. But the right of anyone to open an ale house in return for a small fee led to appalling scenes of inebriation in thousands of little bucket shops known as Tom and Jerry houses. The free traders admitted defeat and the Wine and Beerhouse Act of 1869 once again brought licensing under the control of the magistrates. Other 19th century legislation makes curious reading in these times of severe restrictions on pub opening hours. The Permitted Hours in London Act of 1839 required that all public houses had to close from midnight on Saturday until noon on Sundays. The rest of England and Wales was brought into line in 1848. In 1845 the playing of billiards in pubs was prohibited on Sundays, Christmas Day and Good Friday. In 1853 a more familiar piece of legislation was introduced as a result of pressure from the vociferous temperance movement: all bars in Scotland were closed on the Sabbath. Wales followed suit in 1881. England escaped by a hairbreadth. In the same year a bill to bring Sunday closing to England was given a second reading in the Commons but was finally rejected.

The early years of the 20th century saw concerted efforts by the Liberals and the temperance movement to curb drinking through increased beer duty and other measures. Massive popular opposition and animosity from the House of Lords defeated most of the proposals but David Lloyd George got his revenge during the First World War. As Minister of Munitions and a staunch teetotaller (he was a legend in his own lunchtime, but in the boudoir not the bar) Lloyd George believed that drinking was ruining the war effort. 'Drink is doing us more damage than all the German submarines put together', he declared. The government toyed with the idea of banning drinking but drew back and instead curtailed permitted hours for pubs in 1914. A year later, under the Defence of the Realm Act, it brought in the Central Control Board which administered State Management Schemes in three key areas of munitions production in London, Scotland and, most famously, Carlisle. Under the SMS, breweries and pubs in the areas were effectively nationalised: the idea was to provide low gravity beers in cheerless surroundings that were open for just a few hours a day. Lloyd George drove the legislation through a panicky parliament with blood-curdling and embroidered tales of hordes of drunken munitions workers pouring over the border from Gretna and laying waste to Carlisle's pubs and women. The threat was ever-present because the state-owned brewery and pubs lingered on until 1970 when they were denationalised by the government of Edward Heath. The nationwide restrictions on pub opening hours, introduced as a temporary precaution in 1914, have survived for even longer. They were consolidated in the 1921 Licensing Act which laid down that London pubs could open for nine hours a day and five hours on Sunday. Outside London, pubs were restricted to eight hours a day during the week. The law has been tinkered with but remains on the statute books.

Even though people's life styles, incomes and attitudes to drinking and pub going have changed out of all recognition from the early 1920s, pubs in England and Wales can open for 9½ hours during the week and for just a brief, frustrating 5½ hours on the universal day of rest. Magistrates tend to be generous these days in granting extensions on Friday and Saturday nights but the general, all-pervading attitude is that the Nanny State knows best and we should be prevented from the right to exercise our own judgement and self-control. The main argument against change is that if pubs were allowed to open for longer hours then the populace would go on a bender from which the economy and public morality would never recover. Curiously, this argument does not apply to supermarkets where alcohol is freely available and purchasers are not supervised.

Three attempts by MPs in the 1970s and 80s to introduce private members' bills to amend the law in England and Wales have foundered on the rock of the temperance movement's well-orchestrated filibuster. The latest attempt, in 1987, disappeared into the parliamentary black hole when a bill introduced by Scottish Conservative MP Allan Stewart was 'talked out'. The Queen's Speech in June 1987, however, promised a bill to allow pubs to open for a maximum of 12 hours a day, Monday to Saturday. If the bill is given a 'free vote', it could face major opposition.

England and Wales have some of the most restricted licensing hours in the civilised world and some areas of the Principality are still 'dry' on Sunday. The argument of the opponents of change is a simple one: that greater availability of alcohol leads to greater abuse. The argument is not supported by evidence from other countries, which the anti-alcohol lobby conveniently ignores. Australia is a good example. For years many states had the notorious and unpleasant 'six o'clock swill'. Bars had to close early in the evening and drinkers would descend on bars like locusts to drink them dry before the shutters came down. Now bars can stay open until later in the evening and the evidence is that people now drink in a more civilised fashion. Sweden, on the other hand, which has even more restricted hours than England and Wales, is suffering from a major growth in drink-related problems. As was seen in the United States during Prohibition, if drinkers cannot get supplies then they either make their own or turn to bootleggers.

The argument in support of change has been given powerful support in recent years by the Scottish experience. Scotland used to be notorious for its heavy drinking and the severe restrictions placed on public house hours. They had to shut at 10pm every evening and the 'ten o'clock swill' in big city pubs was not always a pretty sight or a pleasant experience. Bars were shut on Sunday and only 'travellers' could be served a drink in hotels. Dedicated drinkers would hire coaches on Sundays to cross from one side of Aberdeen, Dundee, Glasgow or Edinburgh to the other to prove that they were genuinely on the move. This absurd situation ended in 1976 with the Scotland (Licensing) Act which was based on the recommendations of the Clayson Committee. Dr Christopher Clayson and his team believed that liberalising the licensing laws in Scotland would lead to more relaxed and civilised drinking. Bars can now open on Sundays if licensees seek permission to do so. They can also get permission to have regular afternoon extensions that effectively means that many bars are open from 11am until 11pm. The licensing authorities have also responded generously to applications for late-night extensions and some Scottish bars stay open until long after midnight.

If the opponents of change were right then the social fabric of Scottish society would have been destroyed and there would be riot, pillage and general mayhem on the streets. Nothing of the sort has happened. The Scots have responded to the opportunity to become more civilised. They have shown the brighter not the darker side of human behaviour. In the decade since the new act became law, there has been no increase in the consumption of alcohol and a welcome decline in drink-related offences. The police are enthusiastic supporters of the new system and report that they no longer need to deploy officers in heavy numbers at closing time. It is difficult to base too much evidence on just ten years of change, especially when unemployment has increased sharply in Scotland with a depressive effect on the consumption of alcohol. But the worst fears of the critics have not come about and there is no doubt that Scottish bars are now more pleasant places in which to drink. They are no longer all just 'drinking shops' inhabited by men. I have seen couples coming into bars at four o'clock in the afternoon for a quiet drink – including tea or coffee – after doing the shopping. I have enjoyed a drink at 2am in bars in Edinburgh's Grassmarket where the atmosphere has been relaxed and free from the dreadful menace that too often accompanied drinking in Scotland before the change.

The opponents of change south of the border seem to think that people go to pubs in order to get drunk. Therefore if you extend pub hours people will become more intoxicated. QED. In fact people go to pubs for many complex reasons. They go for a drink – though not necessarily an alcoholic one – for company, for conversation, to play games, to relax after work. Few go to get drunk. Drunks are unpleasant. They spoil other people's pleasure. They are usually thrown out by landlords who stand to lose their licences if they encourage drunken behaviour. Pubs are supervised places in which the moderate consumption of alcohol is encouraged and is the norm. Only a fool would ignore the rising trend of drink-related problems but the blame should not be laid at the door of the public house. The effects of too easy access in supermarkets and glossy, expensive advertising that suggests that social and sexual success are inextricably linked to ordering the 'right' drink should not be overlooked.

Alcohol is a good friend and a bad enemy. Unlike any other social drug, it can be mildly beneficial if taken in moderation. It can also be a killer. I am all in favour of government action to cut consumption. Advice on how many drinks to take each week is sensible and necessary. Curbs on advertising alcohol or at least a voluntary code to remove the 'machismo' image of alcohol should be thoroughly and urgently investigated. But it is a nonsense to suggest that Britain is awash with drink. On the

CHAPTER THIRTEEN

Last orders

A beery voyage of discovery through Britain finds a great profusion of tastes – and the great north-south divide of serving ale with or without a foaming head.

The little pub in the Yorkshire dales was packed that Sunday. The quiet hum of conversation and rumble of laughter were punctuated by the plonk of darts finding their target. On the bar two stubby, black handpumps stood like sentinels and offered the simple choice of mild or bitter. We ordered bitter but my soft, southern tastebuds were not expecting the assault of rich tastes, the subtle creaminess of malt overlaid by the sharp tingle of hops. It was the early 1970s and London was awash with heavily trumpeted keg beers that I found unpalatably cold and carbonated. Now I had refound the pleasures of beer. My friend, more knowledgeable than me, said: 'This is real ale'. At the time, the expression was more an affirmation of quality than a description of a beer style but it was sufficient to send me on a personal voyage of discovery. That first taste had been Theakston's bitter, brewed at the time in the small Yorkshire market town of Masham. I found that 'real ale' was not confined to the north. A change of office in London brought me a few yards from a Young's pub, the Rose and Crown in Hackney. It was the obvious place to congregate after work. Here again were those welcoming sentinels on the bar, not the garish boxes that dispensed Watney's Red or Tavern Keg or Worthington E in most of the surrounding pubs. Young's bitter, which I quickly learnt to call by its curious Cockney nickname of 'ordinary', is a shockingly bitter yet fruity beer, the last remaining example of the true well-hopped London bitter.

From the press I started to read of the activities of the fledgling Campaign for Real Ale while Richard Boston's weekly column on beer in the *Guardian* reinforced CAMRA's complaints about the grip of giant breweries and the uphill struggles of independent firms to keep their hopes and their beers alive. New tastes, new joys came thick and fast now. A visit to Suffolk took in the friendly little coastal town of Southwold, its inshore lighthouse beckoning like a stubby whitewashed finger across the marshes. In the Red Lion on the green I had my first pint of Adnams' bitter. The tangy taste with, I swear, a hint of seaweed marked this out as something special. Regular visits to Southwold became necessary for Adnams has to be drunk close to home. It does not travel and its subtleties of taste are somehow flattened and lost in the London free trade.

A weekend in Ludlow introduced the delights of Robinson's best bitter. The Wheatsheaf, a handsome little pub built into the city's walls, had a vast array of keg fonts on its bar and a solitary handpump serving the beer from Stockport. I had planned a tour of the town's pubs but I remained in the Wheatsheaf, marvelling as the 'Robbies' slipped effortlessly down. I had a similar experience in a hotel high above the awesome sweep of Robin Hood's Bay in Yorkshire. At first I thought I had made a mistake and booked into a keg-only establishment, for a white box not a reassuring handpump announced Cameron's best bitter on the bar. It was an early meeting with an electric pump. One taste of the smooth, nutty bitter was enough for me to decide that beer not wine would accompany lunch and dinner, and only a decent upbringing prevented me from drinking it at breakfast too.

When profession and pastime merged as editor for six memorable if hazy years of the *Good Beer Guide* I had the good fortune to visit on a regular basis printers in Edinburgh and a designer in Manchester. In the Scottish capital I unravelled the mysteries of light, heavy and air pressure dispense. In Bennet's magnificent tiled Victorian bar in Leven Street, the remarkable braw atmosphere of the Diggers – the Athletic Arms – and the snooty elegance of the Café Royal I found three of the finest pubs in Britain. Belhaven's 80 shilling ale was and is a rich beery delight. In the ten years that I have known the company it has gone through almost constant upheaval and changes of ownership. For a time it was owned by Mr Eric D. Morley, better known for his stewardship of the Miss World competition. One holder of the title even posed beside the Belhaven mash tun in the obligatory bathing suit. In spite of such distractions, Belhaven beer has retained its remarkable virtues. In Manchester choice and quality had evaded the clutches of the brewing giants. Here was an astonishing abundance of beers sold at such give-away prices that I thought at first the breweries must be subsidised by the rates. Boddingtons, Lees, Hydes and Holts, with Robinsons down the road in Stockport, provide an array of tastes that tempt you to think that the Big Six either do not exist or that Manchester lives in a personal time warp where the laws of the market economy do not apply.

The more you travel the barley-strewn highways and byways of Britain the more you are forced to conclude that this small island, half the size of France, has as many brewing pleasures as the French have vinous ones. The West Country has a sensible range of light bitters from such companies as Devenish, Hall and Woodhouse and Whitbread's Cheltenham plant that are known somewhat dismissively as 'boy's bitters' and yet which pack great taste and character into their low gravities. At the other end of the hydrometer, Greene King's leg-trembling Abbot Ale from Suffolk is one of the wonders of the brewing age, defying the natural sweetness of strong beers by circulating over a deep bed of hops for several weeks when fermentation is finished. Fuller's ESB from west London is even stronger and regularly walks away with the top prizes at beer festivals and tastings as judges marvel at its great depth and roundness of taste. Lesser known and lighter beers stick in my mind. At one CAMRA beer festival, with an enormous variety of ales on offer, I found Felinfoel's bitter from Wales, a beer that lived in the shadow of its better known, stronger stablemate Double Dragon. It seemed perverse, but while others attempted to sample every beer in view, I stuck to Felinfoel's succulent brew for the duration.

In the Midlands no trip to Trent Bridge is complete without smuggling a 'carry keg' of Home bitter into the ground to watch the cricket. I like, too, the creamy smoothness of Banks's bitter and the hint of sweetness in Ansells, especially their dark mild. Mitchells and Butlers and Shipstone's brews have never impressed me but there is choice enough to make up for the occasional disappointments. From Yorkshire Sam Smith's Old Brewery bitter is one of the most famous cask beers around and yet its attributes have passed me by. But that great region has other pleasures in store, including the bitter-sweet joys of Tetley, the dazzling quality of Timothy Taylor's brews from Keighley and the malty delights of Ward's bitter. As a resident of the other 'north', the Home Counties above London, I must not ignore such splendid brews as Brakspear's and Wethered's hoppy ales from the Thames Valley and Hook Norton's biscuity bitter from its fine tower brewery in the village of the same name. I am also a devotee of the tawny bitter produced by Charles Wells from their modern Legoland plant in Bedford, a beer that divides drinkers' loyalties more than any I know. While I rush salivating to a Charlie Wells' pub, others rush palpitating in the opposite direction. I console myself in the belief that good taste must necessarily be confined to far-sighted iconoclasts.

Whenever I hear politicians speak of the 'north-south' divide my immediate reaction is to assume they are referring to the way in which beer is served. In the north, Yorkshire in particular, they like a thick collar of foam on their beer, possibly as a result of the high levels of carbonation produced in the Yorkshire square fermenting system. I have always thought this dedication to foam curious, especially when you consider that Yorkshire people have a deserved reputation for being careful with their money. A thick head on beer not only gets up your nose and in the way of the liquid you want to drink, but all too often it fails also to give you a full pint in your glass. Bar staff bend double with effort as they labour over beer pumps to deliver pints with their thick collars. A small nozzle called a sparkler is attached to the end of the tap. Inside the sparkler there is a small circle of perforated wire, similar to the ones in those old-fashioned rubber spouts that used to be attached to kitchen taps to direct the water in a firm, strong jet. When the beer flows through the sparkler, it is churned and eddied, forcing the natural carbonation of the beer to create the head of foam. In the Hartlepool area in the North-East they go to even greater lengths to get a head on the beer. In Cameron's pubs I have seen each pint pulled through two separate handpumps. The first tap has such a tight sparkler that all the beavering barman can do is produce half a glass of foam. He then tops the glass up from the second tap which has no sparkler attached. All of this effort in the north means that a lot of beer runs over the top of the glass when it is being filled. The spilt beer is not wasted. It is recycled through a device known as an economiser and served again with the next pull of the pump. The economiser is under attack from the health authorities.

In the soft south we do not worry about the size of the head. It is a northern fabrication to suggest, however, that us effete softies are so cushioned from the harsh realities of life that we don't mind if our beer is flat. Beer that is quite devoid of any foam is clearly out of condition and should be returned to the bar with a careful, more-in-sorrow-than-in-anger remark to the effect that 'this is not quite right today – but it was in splendid nick last night'. This must be said with a deference that will avoid your being summarily and painfully dumped on the pavement outside. Beer pulled through a sparkler-free tap will have a natural, thin head on it that will slowly disappear as you get on with the serious business of supping the liquid. There is no doubt that the style of delivery does have a marked effect on the beer. Barrie Pepper, a splendidly rotund and stalwart CAMRA member from Leeds, once asked the landlord of a pub in St Albans if he had a tight sparkler. The guv'nor rummaged in an old box, found one and screwed it on. The pints he then pulled had a noticeably softer and creamier character. Another St Albans landlord would greet a CAMRA official who came from the north by putting on a tight sparkler and ostentatiously producing a pint with such a vast head that it stood clear of the glass like Herbert Morrison's quiff.

There is as much debate and division about the ideal shape of the beer glass as there is about the size of the head. This debate has little to do with north versus south. It is more of a class divide, with working class drinkers tending to prefer thin 'straight' glasses, while the middle class go for 'jugs' with handles. At this very moment someone is probably writing an earnest thesis on the subject for a redbrick university. I prefer a straight glass because it is lighter to hold but I don't object if I am given a jug and I am slightly embarrassed when drinkers in my company make a great thing of demanding straight glasses. A few years ago an attempt was made to bridge the cultural divide with a new glass known, rather unfortunately, as a 'dimpled straight'. It did not last long even in these sexually enlightened times. The last word on the subject of beer containers was said by a CAMRA member interviewed for television in a pub. Asked why he was holding a jug with his hand round the main body of the glass and the handle pointing away from him, he did not pause or even blink. 'Because if the handle breaks, all I lose is the handle,' he said.

All the concern for foaming heads and shapes of glasses pales into insignificance alongside the fact that in Britain we have a type of beer that is brilliant both in its unique method of production and in the glorious profusion of its tastes and colours and regional characteristics. Our natural taciturnity means that we do not give our beer the praise and recognition it deserves. Thomas Hardy was an exception. He was so impressed by the beer of Eldridge Pope that he immortalised it in his novel *The Trumpet Major*. The beer of 'Casterbridge' (Dorchester) he said was 'the most beautiful colour that the eye of an artist in beer could desire; full in body, yet brisk as a volcano, piquant, yet without a twang; luminous as an autumn sunset; free from streakiness of taste; but, finally, rather heady. The masses worshipped it, the minor gentry loved it more than wine, and by the most illustrious country families it was not despised. Anybody brought up for being drunk and disorderly in the streets of its natal borough had only to prove that he was a stranger to the place and its liquor to be honourably dismissed

148

by the magistrates as one overtaken in a fault that no man could guard against who entered the town unawares.' Eldridge Pope repaid the compliment by producing the bottle-conditioned Thomas Hardy's Ale, complete with an excerpt from the description on the label.

Fine, mellow words but perhaps a trifle too fulsome for the British palate. I prefer the subtle understatement of a former colleague of mine at CAMRA. David had a rare passion for Charles Wells' bitter. Every lunchtime he would walk all the way across St Albans, passing a dozen pubs or more, to the one house in the city that sold the Bedford bitter. His performance never varied. As he entered the public bar he would raise his finger and Ken the landlord would reach for a pint glass and fill it as David walked to the counter. He never rushed. He looked at the pint for a moment or two, waiting for the beer to settle and the head to form. Then he would reach for the glass and fleetingly hold it up to the light, savouring the crystal clarity and tawny colour of the beer. Then, and only then, would he put the glass to his lips and despatch a good third of the contents. A great explosion of pleasure, a long orgasmic 'Aaaagh!', accompanied the return of the glass to the bar. David would suck the foam from his moustache and then say to the bar and to the world in general all that needed to be said on the subject of the quality, the pleasure, the unalloyed brilliance of his beer:

'Not bad that.'

Plain persons guide to pub and beer terms

Adjunct: brewing materials added to malted barley such as wheat, maize, rice or pasta flour, usually to produce a cheaper beer.

Air pressure: the Scottish system of serving beer. An air compressor (or more rarely a water engine) drives the beer to the bar.

Ale: originally an unhopped beverage brewed from barley, indigenous to the British Isles. Now synonymous with beer and used to denote both a weak beer – mild ale – or a strong one – old ale.

Alpha acid: the main bittering agent of the hop flower.

Artist: drinker with an almost theatrical devotion to alcohol. As in the case of two legendary artists, Robert Newton and Wilfrid Lawson, who were once removed with some difficulty from a pub shortly before curtain up and literally poured into their costumes. Lawson was first on stage and was greeted with hoots and howls of derision as he staggered around the stage. Finally he approached the footlights and grated: 'If you think I'm p★★★★d, wait till you see the Duke of Buckingham.' [see p★★★★d]

Barley: cereal from which malt is made for brewing.

Barley wine: a strong beer with a high gravity, often made for winter drinking.

Beer: alcoholic drink made by fermenting barley malt and other materials, flavoured with hops.

Beer engine: suction pump operated by handpump that draws beer from the cask to the bar. One pull delivers a half-pint.

Bine: climbing stem of the hop.

Bitter: the major British beer style, a well-hopped beer also known as pale ale (usually in bottled form) or IPA – India Pale Ale.

Blanket pressure: a low pressure of carbon dioxide put on cask beer to prolong its life by excluding air. Frowned on by CAMRA as careless use can make the beer fizzy.

Boozer: from Dutch *busen*, to drink. Slang name for a pub or a heavy drinker.

Bottle-conditioned: a beer that undergoes a natural secondary fermentation in the bottle and throws a slight sediment. Worthington White Shield and Guinness Extra Stout are the best known examples, but not all Guinness is now bottle-conditioned.

Bottom fermentation: the lager style of brewing.

Brewery-conditioned: beer that is conditioned in the brewery by chilling, filtering and often pasteurisation. The results are keg, bright and lager beers.

Brewster: old English term for a woman brewer.

Brown ale: bottled form of mild ale.

Bung: hole at flat end of a beer cask to which a tap and pipe are connected to serve beer.

Burtonise: adding salts to water to reproduce the type of water rich in calcium sulphate that is found in Burton-on-Trent and is ideal for brewing bitter beer.

Caramel: roasted sugar added to give dark colour to beer.

Carbon dioxide: gas produced during fermentation by the action of yeast on wort. Natural carbonation is necessary to keep beer in good condition; applied pressure makes beer unpleasantly fizzy.

Cask: generic name for traditional beer container, made either from wood or metal. Sizes of casks are: pin (4½ gallons); firkin (9 gallons); kilderkin (18 gallons); barrel (36 gallons); hogshead (54 gallons).

Cask-conditioned: draught beer allowed to condition and undergo a secondary fermentation in the cask through the action of yeast on sugars in the beer.

Copper: vessel in which wort and hops are boiled prior to fermentation.

Decoction: system of mashing usually applied to lager brewing.

Draught: misused term for all bulk beer. Should strictly be used only to indicate beer that is drawn from cask to bar, not pushed by gas pressure.

Duty: the tax levied on beer by Customs and Excise.

Economiser: type of beer dispenser now confined to north of England. Beer that over-runs the glass is recycled.

Electric pump: simple pump that draws beer to the bar without the manual effort of a beer engine. Found mainly in the Midlands and the north.

Elephant's trunk: Cockney rhyming slang for the state of inebriation.

Entire or **entire butt:** original name for porter, strong dark beer drawn from one cask – entire butt – rather than mixed from three separate ones.

Fermentation: the action of yeast on wort to produce alcohol and carbon dioxide.

Finings (or **isinglass**): substance made from swim bladder of sturgeon, added to beer at conditioning stage to clarify it.

Grist: coarse powder produced when malted barley is 'cracked' in a mill before mashing.

Half 'n half: mixing two beers in one pint glass, such as mild and bitter.

Handpump: popular name for a beer engine but strictly applied it is the lever on the bar that operates the engine. Sometimes known as a handpull in the north.

151

Head: froth on top of beer.

Heavy: Scottish term for beer that is similar to bitter. Also known as 70 shilling.

Home-brew house: pub where the beer is brewed on the premises.

Hop: climbing plant with flowers that adds essential bitterness to beer.

India Pale Ale (IPA): original beer style from Burton-on-Trent designed for India trade, a pale ale of medium to high gravity and heavily hopped. Loosely used today, it should apply only to beers with original gravities of 1045 degrees or higher.

Infusion: simple mashing system used mainly in British Isles for top-fermented beer.

Keg: sealed pressurised container in which brewery-conditioned beer is kept.

Kettle or **brew kettle:** another name for copper.

Kiln: process of heating that halts germination of barley and produces barley malt. A similar process is used to cure hops in an oast house.

Lager: from German word meaning 'to store'. Misused and abused term for beer produced by bottom fermentation, originating in Bohemia and Bavaria.

Lates: beer served by myopic landlord unable to read the clock. Also known in London as 'afters'.

Light ale: bottled version of bitter.

Liquor: brewer's term for water.

Malt: basic ingredient of beer made from partially germinated and kilned barley.

Malt extract: evaporated treacle made from wort and used for home brewing.

Mash: infusion of malt and hot liquor at start of brewing process.

Mash tun: vessel used for mashing.

Mild ale: low gravity beer, usually darker than bitter through use of roasted malt or caramel. Light milds without colouring are also produced.

Milk stout: now defunct term for sweet stout that ran foul of trades description legislation.

Oast house: building in which hops are cured.

Old ale: beer of high gravity usually brewed in winter months.

Original or **starting gravity:** system peculiar to Britain for determining potential strength of beer. Duty is paid on a beer's original gravity, a measure by hydrometer of the 'fermentable materials' (malt, sugar and other cereals) present in the wort before fermentation. Water has a gravity of 1000 degrees so a beer with an 'OG' of 1040 will have 40 parts of fermentable material added to the water. A rough and ready guide is that a 1040 degrees beer is about 4 per cent alcohol, 1050 degrees is 5 per cent alcohol and so on. Beers are now required to indicate their OGs on bottle, can or pump but gravity bandings, i.e. 1040 to 1045 degrees, are used to allow for slight variations from one brew to another.

Pale ale: best or special bitter in bottled form. Sometimes the name of draught beer as well.

Paraflow: heat exchange system that cools hopped wort before fermentation.

Pasteurisation: heat system named after Louis Pasteur that kills living matter in beer. Avoided by skilled brewers as it gives burnt sugar taste to beer.

P★★★★d: vulgar expression that denotes a state of inebriation.

Pished: expression used in polite society in Scotland to indicate that someone has partaken of alcoholic beverage to excess.

Porter: popular name for entire butt beer, forerunner of stout.

Priming: adding sugar solution to beer to encourage secondary fermentation.

Racking: running beer from conditioning tanks into casks. 'Racked bright' is a beer taken off its sediment for quick consumption.

Real ale: popular term for cask-conditioned draught beer.

Roasted barley: unmalted dark barley used to give colour to mild or stout.

Ropy: beer that has a bacterial infection.

Round: British system, now in decline as a result of high price of alcohol, in which members of a group take it in turns to buy a round of drinks. Also known as a shout or standing your corner.

Scotch: Geordie expression for a medium gravity beer, equivalent to 70 shilling or heavy in Scotland.

Secondary fermentation: the continuing action of yeast on sugar either in the cask or the bottle.

Shilling: system of grading beer in Scotland according to now defunct invoice system for casks. 60 shilling is light or mild beer, 70 shilling is heavy and 80 shilling is strong beer.

Shive: opening on top of traditional beer cask through which it is filled and then bunged. The central core is knocked through in the pub cellar to allow the beer to be vented with the use of a spile or wooden peg.

Skimming: removing excess yeast from surface of fermenting wort.

Snob screen: small revolving glass screen on top of Victorian bars to prevent the hoi polloi from seeing their betters in the saloon.

Sparging: washing the spent grains in the mash tun with hot liquor to extract remaining sugars.

153

Sparkler: device fitted to beer tap in the north to generate tight foaming head on beer.

Spile: porous wooden peg fitted into shive hole to allow carbon dioxide to escape from cask.

Square: type of fermenting vessel confined mainly to Yorkshire.

Stout: dark beer brewed from roasted malt and unmalted roasted barley, usually with high hop rate. Successor to porter.

Sulphites: added to beer to prolong its life. Other chemical additives are used to speed fermentation, cut down on yeast head and create a false head on finished beer. British beer, while classified as food, is excluded from labelling requirements to list ingredients. Drinkers allergic to sulphites or benzoates may not be aware that they are present in beer.

Tied house: pub owned by a brewery.

Top fermentation: system mainly confined to British Isles in which yeast acts on top of wort.

Top pressure: system that forces beer to the bar by action of carbon dioxide.

Ullage: waste beer.

Water engine: see air pressure.

Wort: sweet liquid produced by mashing malt and liquor.

Yeast: Single cell fungus that acts on sweet wort to produce alcohol and carbon dioxide.

Zonked: see p★★★★d.

Useful addresses

Brewery museums: The Bass Museum at Burton-on-Trent is in beautifully restored old brewery buildings and has fascinating displays on the history of brewing and pubs, including a former brewery train. It is in Horninglow Street (A50) and is open Monday to Friday, 10.30 to 4.30 and Saturday and Sunday, 11 to 5. Tel: 0283 45301. The Heritage Brewery Museum Trust, also in Burton, is based in the former Everard's Tiger Brewery. It is a working brewery that aims to keep alive the history and traditions of the capital of the British brewing industry. It is a membership organisation. Current membership is £5 a year. Further details from the Heritage Brewery Museum Trust, Heritage Brewery, Anglesey Road, Burton-on-Trent, Staffs DE14 3PF. Tel: 0283 69226.

Many breweries welcome visitors on conducted tours, but tours must be in small parties and booked or arranged well in advance. For details of all British breweries, consult the annual *Good Beer Guide* published by the Campaign for Real Ale. CAMRA is a membership organisation dedicated to preserving traditional British beer and pubs and campaigning against mergers and takeovers that restrict consumer choice. Membership is currently £9 a year. Details from CAMRA, 34 Alma Road, St Albans, Herts AL1 3BW. Tel: 0727 67201.

Sources and further reading

Frank Baillie, *The Beer Drinker's Companion*, David and Charles, 1975.
Richard Boston, *Beer and Skittles*, Collins, 1976.
Campaign for Real Ale, *Licence for Change*, 1985.
H.S. Corran, *A History of Brewing*, David and Charles, 1975.
Ian Donachie, *A History of the Brewing Industry in Scotland*, John Donald, 1979.
Richard Filmer, *Hops and Hop Picking*, Shire, 1982.
Brian Glover, *CAMRA Dictionary of Beer*, Longman, 1985.
Michael Hardman and Theo Bergstrom, *Beer Naturally*, Bergstrom and Boyle, 1976.
Christopher Hutt, *Death of the English Pub*, Arrow, 1973.
Michael Jackson, *World Guide to Beer*, Mitchell Beazley, 1977.
David Keir, *The Younger Centuries*, McLagen and Cumming, 1951.
Cadbury Lamb, *Inn Signs*, Shire, 1976.
Maurice Lovett, *Brewing and Breweries*, Shire, 1981.
Peter Mathias, *The Brewing Industry in England 1700–1830*, Cambridge University Press, 1959.
H.A. Monckton, *A History of the English Public House*, Bodley Head, 1969.
H.A. Monckton, *A History of Ale and Beer*, Bodley Head, 1966.
Roger Protz, *Pulling a Fast One*, Pluto Press, 1978.
John Pudney, *A Draught of Contentment*, New English Library, 1971.
John Watney, *Beer is Best*, Peter Owen, 1974.
The Story of British Beer and *The Story of the British Pub* by H.A. Monckton are available from the Brewers' Society. *The Story of Bass* and *A Glass of Pale Ale, a visit to Burton, 1880*, are available from Bass.
Monopolies Commission and Price Commission reports, Brewing Review, The Brewer, What's Brewing, Good Beer Guide.

Good ale, the true and proper drink of Englishmen.
He is not deserving of the name of Englishman who
speaketh against ale, that is good ale.

George Borrow

ACKNOWLEDGEMENTS

Cover illustration from an idea by Phil Evans.
Photograph of author on back cover: courtesy of Nigel Norie.
Cartoons on pp. 4, 60, 70, 72, 86, 132, 140 and 142 by Phil Evans.
Working brewery drawing on p. 79 by Trevor Hatchett.
Photographs courtesy of Whitbread (p. 36), Bass (pp. 42, 47, 50 and 96),
Michael Jackson (pp. 52, 56 and 57), CAMRA (pp. 62, 84, 89, 99, 101 and
117), Eldridge Pope & Co. (p. 107) and the Brewers' Society (p. 122).